How Not
to Do Things

Susan Blood

Surface Popper Publications

Cape Cod

First published by Surface Popper Publications, June 2017

Surface Popper Publication's books may be purchased for educational, business, or sales promotional use.
www.surfacepopperbooks.com

Cover photograph by Michael and Suz Karchmer.
Cover design by Kristen vonHentschel

ISBN 978-0-9990390-0-7

For Chris, Lucy, and Simon

Contents

Author's Note

When I was a Girl Scout I realized that many badges could be mine by going through the handbook and combing the lists of requirements for things I had already done. For instance, I had made countless outfits for my stuffed mouse Wallis, knew how to replace a button, and had sustained at least one life-threatening sewing injury, so the Sewing badge was essentially mine. In this way I populated my sash by leveraging activities I had inadvertently completed and then polishing off the remaining requirements. It felt like cheating but my sash was awesome.

This book is that sash.

I was driving home one day mulling over possible get-rich-quick schemes when I thought of that story where a prophet asks the widow woman "what hast thou in the house?" In the story, she has a bottle of oil which she pours into Tupperware borrowed from her neighbors and they all live happily ever after. I thought, *what do I have in the house?* I have a couple kids, a husband, a dog, cat, fish, chickens, hamster, and rogue mice (not all at the same time), a bunch of dust bunnies, a rotating list of short and long term guests, and a robot vacuum. I am not allowed to sell any of these things.

Once when we were leaving a meeting my friend Ira made the mistake of asking me how things were going.

"You should write a book," he said when I finally finished talking about how it was going with my mother and mother-in-law both living with us. "People love to read about other people's misery."

On that get-rich-quick drive I realized that if I collected all the stories I had jotted down, I had in fact written a book. Some of these stories were written when my friend wanted a blog for her art gallery and asked me for help. Not wanting to screw something up with her name on it, I started a disposable, practice blog to work out the kinks. I called it Trout Towers after my husband Chris' recording studio, which doubles as the name of our home. In hindsight, I realize that if I had started my own blog on purpose, I would still be agonizing over what to call it.

Envisioning Trout Towers as a Cape Cod version of *Under the Tuscan Sun*, I aimed to fill it with the minutia of life in a fishing/tourist town. It went off the tracks almost immediately, becoming instead – I'm not sure what. It continued as such long after I set up my friend's gallery blog, to my children's chagrin.

In light of the stories I had at my disposal, I thought I would call the book *How to Handle Things*. However, we learn how to handle things by first learning how not to handle things. For instance, never try to catch a falling knife. Examples poured forth like a cruse of oil.

There were of course hurdles. My editor, for instance, had a few issues with my writing style.

"You can't have all these one word paragraphs," he said.

"People have short attention spans and they like lots of white space on the page," I replied. "I'm putting in more."

"You can't do that."

"Can too."

"Can't."

"Can."

"Can't."

"Can."

"Can't."

"Can and did. Look up."

This explains why the editing ends abruptly midway through the book.

Because they feature prominently in the stories I told my family what I was doing and asked if they wanted to appear as themselves or adopt aliases. My son shrugged his shoulders.

"I'm okay with whatever," he said amicably. That night when I sat down to work the first sentence I read was "He was wearing nothing but a pair of ruby slippers." I changed his name.

My daughter then asked what I would call the book.

"I'm thinking about *How Not to Do Things*," I said.

"Wow," she replied. "We have a lot of material."

How not to maintain a vehicle

When we were married Chris and I had a prenuptial agreement clearly stating that if we should part, he had to keep the Jaguar. He loved it. I did not. Aside from being extraordinarily comfortable, it had no redeeming qualities whatsoever and stood for everything I did not want in a car. Specifically, it was unreliable, greedy, and had entitlement issues.

It was the Jaguar we took to Maine for a weekend getaway as newlyweds – a decision we regretted just north of Boston. The car, I mean. We regretted taking the car.

Chris was driving and to me it felt like he was arbitrarily taking his foot off the gas, making the car lurch when I least expected it. I couldn't imagine why he would do this, but we had only been married a month or so and who knew what oddities he had up his sleeve? Chris assured me that it was the car, not him, and called his mechanic – the one on speed-dial. His mechanic could do nothing, but weighed in with "why on earth would you take *that car* on a road trip?" Chris bought the Jaguar through him, but with full disclosure that it was mostly ornamental.

Lurching up the coast, we discovered that if we kept the gas tank topped off the engine would stop cutting out. Patting ourselves on the back for our automotive genius, we continued to Maine without mishap. We had a lovely few days in Bar Harbor, where we visited friends, watched the sunrise, and ate two breakfasts a day because one was included with our room. We loved Bar Harbor and felt quite at home. When you live in a tourist area, it's great to descend on someone else's town for a change and see what it's like to not know where you're driving.

We took a leisurely drive home, stopping for lunch in Camden. I asked that we lock the car – a request Chris mocks me for to this day. In our family it is not called Camden, it's "the crime-ridden town of Camden." If you have never been there, it is like a postcard. But I had new coffee cups and a couple of "Smile you're in Bar Harbor!" sweatshirts in that car and I was not going to lose them to some Lilly Pulitzer-wearing hoodlum. The car was not broken into and we merrily continued on to Portland, where we stopped because we had heard it was great and we wanted to explore. Also, the car was doing the lurching thing again and we needed gas.

It took Chris a really, really long time to pump the gas, which is not completely surprising since it's a Jaguar and has a 65 gallon tank, giving it a range of 64 miles. Still not finished, he looked in the window and said, "honey, we have a problem." Because Chris is Chris and we had never had new $5 coffee mugs in the car, the Jaguar had never been locked. So we did not know that when you hit the automatic door lock it secured everything including the trunk. Okay, we did know that because we are not idiots. What we didn't know is that the only key Chris had for the Jaguar was a valet key.

Why is this important? When the gas tanks rusted out because of course they did, Chris' mechanic replaced them with a new gas tank which he put in the trunk. With the trunk locked, we had no way to put gas in the car. AAA was of no help whatsoever, since we were neither locked out of the car nor out of gas (although I assured them we would be out of gas before long). They recommended we call a locksmith, which we did.

Since Chris was driving while I talked to the locksmith, he didn't realize that the only locksmith we were able to reach was not able to help us. They only did commercial jobs, not Jaguar trunks. So Chris kept driving toward the locksmith shop while the locksmith tried to help me figure out where else we could go. Eventually I interrupted him with "we're here, do you mind if we come in?" It was after 5:00 p.m. at this point, so he came out to us. And then, because locksmithing is in his blood, he took a look at the car. And then, because he is a locksmith, he tried to open it. For three hours he tried to open it. Finally, he said "I'm going to have to drill the lock." Never have such musical words been spoken in the English language.

We filled the tank and headed home, with mugs accounted for and our marriage intact. It's good to find out early on in a marriage how you deal with crisis as a couple. That way when you find yourselves locked out of an apartment in Manhattan at 2:00 a.m. a year later, you know your spouse is on your team.

I think my trouble with cars is me. My track record has not been great, beginning with my first car, a Volkswagen GTI.

I was admittedly a little wide-eyed when I bought the GTI. I didn't have a terribly good job but had high hopes and expectations. I also didn't realize that it was a bad idea for a car payment to be more than half your monthly income. Fortunately my other expenses were small and I was able to limp along – until things started breaking.

The first thing that went was the passenger side door handle. It was a minor mechanical problem that was probably really easy to fix yet exorbitantly expensive. I put off fixing it because climbing through from the passenger side really wasn't that big a deal. The only time it was a problem was when I had to lock my car.

When I lived at a ski resort, in a pristine town full of joy, snow, and brotherly love, my car was broken into. I came out one morning to go to work and discovered glass all over my driver's seat. It took me a moment to realize what had happened because I lived in utopia and who would do this? Once I came to grips with my broken

3

window I also realized that my stereo was gone, as well as a package headed to the post office containing a mix tape, *Interview with the Vampire*, and a Sesame Street book light. I hope the thief enjoyed them.

Before choosing to smash my driver's side window, the thief tried both forcing the passenger side lock and opening my sunroof like a can of Spam. I was already in hot water with my insurance company. Within the first year of car ownership I was broadsided coming out of my driveway on a little mountain road. I also forgot to set my emergency brake in the parking lot at work once and came out to find my car nose-down an embankment, thankfully not on a picnicking family. So I called and said "hypothetically, if your car is broken into is that your fault?" For reasons I don't recall clearly but I'm sure made sense at the time, I had the window replaced but left the passenger lock and the sunroof in their dysfunctional states. It may be bad luck to open an umbrella in a house, but having one in the car is really handy when your roof leaks. I stopped locking my car because paperbacks are cheaper than windows and climbing in through the hatchback was both cumbersome and embarrassing.

I made a friend on Cape Cod whose business was Bugs, Busses, and Things. He loved all things Volkswagen and took good care of my rolling money pit. "Paul," I'd say. "My car is possessed." He'd then tell me to stuff something under the brake pedal when it was parked to keep the brake lights from coming on at night and killing the battery. My calls to AAA were so increasingly desperate and frequent that once when I started telling them how to get to my unmarked street address, they stopped me. "We know where you live," the dispatcher said.

When I moved, Paul found a buyer for the car. I wanted someone who would love it like I did, faults and all. Paul assured me he had known this guy for years and helped me make the sale. As my GTI peeled out of Bugs, Busses, and Things for the last time Paul looked after it and said "that car is not long for this world." I blew it a kiss and cashed the check.

When I bought the GTI I had recently returned from Germany, where I spent a year deciding who I would be when I grew up and what I would drive when I got there. The GTI was perfect. It was fast, but looked completely unassuming. It was *so me*. My next car, a Saturn, was cheap to buy, cheap to repair, and cheap to insure. It was everything I wanted. It was the new me.

To be fair, even my extremely sensible and fuel efficient car has its moments. On Tuesday my car wouldn't start. On Thursday my car wouldn't stop. Wednesday, as usual, was somewhere in between.

When my car wouldn't start I was waiting to meet a friend I had invited to go to the theater. I'm sure he wasn't at all suspicious when he drove up and I asked him to drive. His car is clean and comfy and I would totally fake a dead car if the opportunity came up again. On Thursday I was on my way to work and when I stopped to run an errand, I couldn't get the ignition to turn off. After a few seconds of hand-wringing and driving back and forth through town like a squirrel at a four-way-stop, I pulled over and called the dealership to let them know I was on my way to see them. While I am not prone to stalling my manual transmission, there is something disconcerting about driving through stop-and-go traffic with a car you can't start if it stalls (the key wouldn't budge in either direction). And did I mention I was almost out of gas? You're not supposed to fill your tank without turning off your engine. Even I know that. So now in addition to keeping my tank full when anyone I know is pregnant, I have to keep my tank full in case my car won't stop driving. My car is a cross between *The Red Tent* and *The Red Shoes*.

They couldn't look at my car right away, so I dropped it off and went to breakfast. When I returned I settled into the waiting room and pretended to read. How often do you get to simply be where you are? The woman at the dealership said sometimes people stay in the waiting room after their cars are finished. I'm thinking of kicking that up a notch and making it a part of my daily routine. The next time I am in the market for a car, I'l make my decision based on the quality of the waiting room. It will be the new me.   cute

How not to catch a mouse

What goes bump, thumpity thump, (pause), crash in the night? Hunter, catching a mouse in the living room. Or maybe importing and releasing a mouse into the living room. It's hard to tell.

I was sitting in the north wing of the Towers late one night when I heard aforementioned crashing. In a moment of previously undiscovered bravery I went out to investigate, thinking to myself "this could be a big mistake." And it was. The aptly named Hunter gave me a look over his shoulder as he trotted past with something in his mouth. And then he put it down, so it could run into the toy corner and hide under the rolling green caterpillar.

The old me would have been all "cute little mouse! Bad cat!" I would have chucked Hunter outside, caught the mouse and relocated it, all the while playing classical music and filling the air with essence of lavender to help the mouse relax. The new me envisioned the following scenarios:

1. Cat catches and decapitates mouse, leaving corpse in middle of living room rug.

2. Cat catches and eats mouse, vomiting corpse in middle of living room rug.

3. Cat fails to catch mouse and I

3a. find it in the drawer under my stove

3b. find signs of it under my stove

3c. discover that it's written home and invited all its friends and relations to live under my stove.

I moved the rolling green caterpillar. Hunter wasn't looking, so I also moved the school bus, which started playing "the wheels on the bus go round and round!" with such gusto it got the attention of the cat and temporarily paralyzed the mouse. The mouse did not remain paralyzed, though, and dashed behind the basket of magnetic building pieces, where it no doubt pondered "what is this sudden redistribution of ions in my little mouse body? I feel a sudden surge of oxygen flow and increased circulation!"

And then it ran for its life again. After I moved the orange front-end loader, the stacking blocks with friendly and familiar images, the sparkly purple skipper and a remote control race car, the mouse made its last mistake and ran between the cat's legs - from back to front - ending at the business end. I had left the door open and Hunter dashed out with his prey again in his mouth – after half the neighborhood had moved in through the open door.

Every winter we have indisputable signs of mice in the house. Signs like actual mice dancing the tarantella in the middle of the kitchen floor. And mouse poop in the cat's water bowl. I don't happen to be lying about the water bowl.

Since we are raging pacifists, we decided not to poison them or sticky tape them or suck them up in the Shop Vac, although the Shop Vac was very, very tempting. Since Hunter has proved himself only partially useful, we got a Havahart trap, rather than smashing their brains out their ears. It has since occurred to me that smashing their brains out their ears may be the more humane route, but I'll get to that. We put some peanut butter in the trap, *et voila*! We caught our first mouse. And then we caught another one. And then the trap got all excited, or maybe nervous, and started snapping at everything that walked by. Including dust.

Meanwhile, we grew concerned about the possibility of having one mouse that just kept coming back for peanut butter. A friend said she put nail polish on her mice before releasing them. Have you ever looked carefully at a mouse's toenails? She must have had a very steady hand and maybe an ether-soaked rag. Being unskilled at mouse pedicures, we figured we'd just take them a reasonable distance away. "Reasonable distance" is of course open to interpretation. There's an old joke about two guys hiking in the woods. They see a bear and one guy puts on his running shoes. The other guy goes "you don't really think those shoes are going to help you outrun that bear, do you?" and running shoe guy says "no, I just have to outrun you."

Which is my way of saying we're letting the mice loose in our neighbors' yards. This is easier than Firefly's suggestion of blindfolding the mouse, spinning it around several times and then driving it to the mainland.

One night after Chris had gone to work I noticed the trap had shut. I was pretty sure it had been set off by more dust so I grabbed the trap to reset it – literally scaring even more poop out of the mouse inside. I texted "MOUSE!!!!!" to Chris but he did not cancel the show where he was a sound engineer and come running home to save me. Which left me in a bit of a pickle. I couldn't leave the mouse in the trap until Chris got home because it would surely communicate the dangers of the trap to its friends and family. We can't let this kind of information circulate. I didn't want to release it myself because while I'm not afraid of mice, I am afraid of rabid coyotes and pretty much everything else in the woods across the street. I didn't want to leave the kids alone in the house and then, inevitably, get eaten by an angry skunk. They're vicious, you know.

But I really couldn't let the mouse sit there warning the others. So I took it out. In the dark. And put it in Chris' Jaguar. Which should teach him not to ignore my texts.

However! Data tells us that when you release a mouse there is a very good chance it will return if you don't take it far enough away. Note: If at some point in the future you are listening to NPR and hear a story about how the Cape Cod fishing industry was destroyed by mice, please deny having read this book.

I asked Google how far you have to take a mouse so it doesn't find its way home, and the general consensus was pretty far. A couple miles far. In my favorite comment stream (which is completely worth reading), one person noted: "They will find their way back unless you sing *Born Free* while releasing them." I was doing that already.

From the sound of things, mice should be released about two miles away. The harbor is less than that but the route involves mouse obstacles (ponds, etc) so we figured it would do the trick. It also seemed like a nice place for mice to live. For bonus points, there's a church at the harbor so I think the mice are a tax deduction. I got some strange looks in the parking lot when I arrived with a mouse to release, so I moved to the other side of the harbor – the untouristy side. It's a little scrappier over there. When I go at night, I can't help but think of *On the Waterfront*.

The mice are reluctant to get out of the trap, but once they do they all go running off in the same direction – which makes me worry that I've created a non-indigenous mouse colony where the fishing boats will be in the summer. I imagine all the buoys sinking because they've been hollowed out by mice and filled with...whatever it is mice like that doesn't float. When you hear about it on NPR, let me know what it is they put in there. Probably rice. Or sheep.

It has also occurred to me that the distance you need to drive the mouse is less about how far away it needs to go before it decides to relocate, and more about increasing its odds of getting eaten. Now that I think of it, if a mouse shows up with our particular shade of nail polish, we should throw it a party. Furthermore, I fear that one day we will find ourselves tied up, Gulliver-style, and relocated to the harbor by an angry horde of mice. They were here first and have indigenous rights.

I hope they at least paint our nails.

How not to renovate your home

Our house has always been something of a three ring circus. Or maybe a french farce. Or a fire drill at a french circus. There are comings and goings at all hours of the day and night and no one ends up where they started. Part of this is because Chris is a sound engineer, so we have musicians in and out of the house on a regular basis. You know that advice you hear about not making it too quiet for a baby since they're used to a lot of noise before they're even born? We recorded a rock album here when Firefly was an infant.

The other part of the circus is that our house has been home to different people at different times. It is a two story house, with a full apartment on the second floor that would be a mother-in-law apartment if my mother-in-law, Ruth, could climb the stairs. For years, we lived upstairs and she lived downstairs. And all was well. Eventually, however, the upstairs apartment got too small for the four of us. It had one large bedroom, plus a wide spot which we convinced the kids was a bedroom until they literally outgrew it (picture Alice as the mushroom kicks in). At approximately the same time, Ruth went from being legally blind to completely blind, and it became apparent that we needed to remove the separation of church and state and combine the upstairs and downstairs.

As all of this was happening, our fabulous friends Liz and Randy desperately needed to get out of their short-term rental while they house hunted. In that moment the love in our hearts yelled louder than the sense in all of our heads and we invited them to move in upstairs – which meant we needed to move out of the upstairs completely and commit to living in a part of the house I had long tried to avoid.

Without going into a great deal of detail, I will say that the downstairs was inhabited by a legally blind person for many years. In the spirit of "don't do unto others as you would prefer they not do unto you," I will not describe the project we walked into, but I will mention – as a tiny example – that we removed a beach bucket of thumbtacks from the walls and about a thousand single serve applesauce cups.

Remember how you moved out of your parents' house but left stuff behind, expecting it to be there when you needed it? Everyone has lived in our house, and they have all left things. In preparing the downstairs for our arrival, I was reminded of that prank in college wherein we stapled Dixie cups together to cover the floor and filled them all half-way with water. Every time I went downstairs to work, I saw some version of those Dixie cups which needed to be dealt with before anything else could be done, with the added complication that someone might want to keep the Dixie cups once we got them all unstapled.

The floors needed to be refinished, which we couldn't do until the furniture/coffee cups/random unclaimed possessions were moved out of the rooms. We couldn't paint the walls until the floors were done. We couldn't move our stuff in until the floors and walls were done. We couldn't move everything we owned out into the yard and just burn it already because the fire department refused to issue us a burn permit, no matter how nicely we asked. It's like they know us or something.

Since there was no place to put things I started making piles in the available space, such as it was. Ruth had very predictable paths through the house which helped her know where she was and from which she did not stray. So I built walls and tunnels with economy boxes of trash bags, toilet paper, and other dry goods. Those of us

13

who could see felt like white mice, minus the cheese at the end of the maze.

Our hall bathroom – the one everyone uses – had all the charm of a crack house. Chris had ripped out drywall and fixed the ceiling, but it still had a certain *je ne sais quoi* which only curling linoleum and rusted fixtures can impart. So my sister gave me a sink from IKEA and now we live in a Swedish crack house. When the plumber came to put it in, I said something like "man, you should have seen the old sink" and he said "lady, *I have seen your sink*." I don't know what he meant by that, but it didn't sound flattering.

Even before we offered the upstairs to our friends, we had decided it would keep us all more sane if we used the downstairs kitchen instead of cleaning and stocking two kitchens – ours (up), and my mother-in-law's (down). As usual, this is the royal we, and *we* made sure to stomp our not so tiny feet and demand a more pleasant atmosphere in the downstairs kitchen before *we* would deign to put our hand-painted pottery on its shelves. We may have tossed our hair and stood with our backs to the offending cabinets, stony-faced. So we (Chris) got an estimate for ripping out everything (including a wall) and replacing everything with shiny! new! appliances, cabinetry, floors and hopefully a new lemon zester as I had lost mine. When I came home that day, I found him on the couch breathing into a paper bag. Which was actually good because suddenly it occurred to me that it would perhaps not be so easy for a blind person (such as my mother-in-law) to find her way around the kitchen once we had put the sink where the stove was and an alligator pit where the refrigerator used to be. She did quite well finding what she needed. Can you imagine if we arbitrarily shifted the contents of all the drawers? Diabolical. So after days of kitchen planning, Chris and I both came to the conclusion that it was not to be.

Or was it? Chris figured we could at least put in a new kitchen floor as the old floor was literally three different kinds of linoleum taped together. We priced flooring and installation on the very cheapest floor we could find, since we would be ripping it all up for the renovation down the line, and discovered we would essentially be stapling 1,300 one dollar bills to the floor and then urethaning them. Except that the aforementioned floor treatment would be more visually appealing than the commercially available flooring we would get with the same money. That's right. The cheapest, most ghastly linoleum floor on the market would be $1,300. In other words, my kitchen asked me to marry it but didn't give me a ring and wouldn't commit to a date. It did, however, suggest we live together first and see how it goes.

I focused my efforts elsewhere. There's a saying about how once you get Cape Cod sand in your shoes you always want to come back. I'm sure the same could be said for using a power sander on Cape Cod. You would totally want to hang out at our house if you came and spent a day sanding.

Chris borrowed a huge sander from his friend and accidentally let me use it once. Our ceilings and walls are still wondering what hit them. If you are moving into a house where a smoker and an ill-trained dog lived, do yourself a favor and get a power sander. It is mind-boggling what a difference it makes, plus it makes you look like Sigourney Weaver when you carry it around.

Whenever Chris wasn't looking I used his random orbit sander. This is mostly notable because until we tackled the house, I didn't know what a random orbit sander was. My arms went numb almost instantly, but I had no intention of stopping. Why clean something when you can sand off the muck? Everywhere I looked, there was something to be sanded. The cat kept a low profile.

I used the sander when Chris wasn't looking because the date our friends needed to get out of their apartment was getting close and Chris took the opportunity to be a perfectionist about everything. Usually I'm the one being nit-picky, but I really wanted the upstairs nice for Liz and Randy and it couldn't be nice with all our stuff strewn everywhere. Every time I announced that it was perfect(ly good enough), Chris would say it just needed one more round of sanding and painting.

I got to the point where I dreamt about the move several times each night. No wonder I was so tired all the time. The upside, however, was that I knew exactly where everything went when I woke up.

Once the kitchen shelves were sanded into submission and repainted, I couldn't wait to move our dishes and food downstairs. I figured once we got settled in for real we could be kosher since we'd have a kitchen both upstairs and downstairs. Can you be kosher if you're not Jewish? If not we have a vegan/non-vegan kitchen. The one we don't use is the vegan one.

I have a theory about how to get things done without knowing you're doing them. Chris once told me about a college campus where they planted grass everywhere and then put walkways where the grass was worn into paths. Likewise, I moved the food downstairs because we like to eat and I figured if the food was down there, we would follow it. It was totally brilliant because that's what we're trying to do in the long run. It was totally not brilliant because there were paint cans and electric drills and vacuum attachments and seven kinds of paint rollers/brushes on the kitchen counters, leaving a 6.5" x 6.25" space to work. Also there was a pile of stuff – boxed kitchen appliances, contents of cupboards, etc. – in the center of the kitchen. Sort of a kitchen island from hell, located well out of the worn walkways.

In hindsight it was the worst of both worlds. Downstairs there was sheetrock dust everywhere. Upstairs was piled with stuff on its way downstairs. At dinner Ruth apologized for spilling something on the floor and I was all, "*like it matters.*"

Four days before our friends were due to move in, and one day before his first day of preschool, Sketch decided he was potty trained. This is a phenomenon completely unrelated to both the renovation and my months of begging and bribing. In the end, he just did it.

This is a recurring lesson for me. I agonize over whatever is not potty trained (because really that's what it all comes down to, right?). The excrement will go where it is supposed to go when it is supposed to go there. When will I learn? I had to let go and know the whole moving thing would happen in its right time, with or without my agonizing over it. I took a deep breath and let it all go.

And then I began hyperventilating because we had *four days* to be out of the upstairs so our friends could move in. Four. That's a day per family member. Life lessons and inner peace were going to have to wait at least long enough for a functioning bathroom.

I'm not including pictures because I don't want to make you sad that you don't have a bathroom like ours. I also don't want to hurt the feelings of whoever picked out the linoleum in the '70s.

If I did, you would notice that the wall around the faucet area of the shower was exposed sheetrock. This is because a couple years ago the people who were staying downstairs objected to being scalded every time someone upstairs (me) took a shower/flushed the toilet/ran the kitchen sink just to hear the screaming. So we had a plumber come and take our house apart to access and remove the scald mechanism. He did not put our house back together when he was done.

However! I asked for a new tile floor for my birthday, and Chris threw in the tile in the shower for good measure. Actually, he wasn't home when The Tile Guru came by, so I asked that it be included in the estimate. You'd think he'd learn. The most pathetic part of getting a tile floor for my birthday is how much time I spent sitting on the bathroom floor admiring it. Italian tile! It's like getting a whole room of pottery.

Unrelated to the work in the bathroom, Chris found a puddle in the basement, so he checked on all the usual, leaky, suspects. Usually it's the pipes behind the washing machine. Those pipes are to be thanked for the stellar education afforded the children of our plumber. Also, the plumber's dog will now be able to go to college.

Those pipes were not leaking. So Chris checked a few other things, which were also not leaking. But he was getting close, by golly, so he investigated our bathroom wall by drilling a two inch diameter hole in the drywall.

Hmmm, not there. How 'bout here? Nope, not there, either. Maybe here?

Here?

No, here?

Here?

Here?

Here?

Here?

Here?

Here...

I am adding "Swiss cheese filigree effect" to my wall treatment board on Pinterest. It will be the next big thing.

Despite Chris' desire to have everything perfect yet inexplicably full of holes, we settled for a semi-renovated bathroom. Chris stripped the walls, removed the lights from where they were thumbtacked to the wall, replaced some circa 1950s accessories more suited to a warehouse bathroom, and put up new sheet rock over the bathtub before the upstairs neighbors had a chance to drop their toothbrushes through the floor and onto our heads while we showered.

The night before our friends had to move out of their rental, we moved into our downstairs bedroom. Earlier that day I was chatting with a group of moms and had to dash because I was Very Busy Moving. One of the moms said, "you know, you can hire people to do that for you." And it's true, I could. Except I'm a New Englander and it really irks me to pay people to do things *not as well* as I would do them. Besides, I have no idea where things go and if someone else moved us, well, we'd never find anything ever again. Note: There is a point at which you do not care if you never find anything again.

I think everyone should move out of part of their house for a little while. For one thing, it makes entire ant populations disband. And for another, I found my lemon zester. Finding my lemon zester makes the fact I could barely lift my arms all worthwhile. I lacked the strength to zest a lemon, but at least I had the tool.

Right about the time the Upstairs Neighbors started moving in, carrying things up the outside staircase while we were moving things down the inside staircase, the VNA came to help Ruth. Come to think of it, she might have been there all along and we didn't notice her because the living room was filled almost completely with things to be placed in rooms and drawers and cupboards and donation bins. So many places to hide.

The VNA came on and off to help Ruth with her personal care – showering, and whatnot. They also helped her pick out clothes, which offends me personally because I usually did that for her and have there been complaints?

We chatted in the dining room for a bit and then she asked to see Ruth's bathroom, to make sure it was safe for her. I led her through the storage area/living room and could only imagine what she was thinking. Also the kitchen counters were piled sky-high with pans and Tupperware looking for new homes. Sky. High.

The VNA looked relieved when she saw Ruth's bathroom. She may also have wondered how a blind person was managing to get around amid the mayhem. And the answer to that would be, cheerily. Ruth loved the chaos. She discovered we had piled heaps and heaps of things on either side of her usual paths, which made her laugh at us and go about her business as though nothing ridiculous was going on.

Our end game was to give the kids their own rooms downstairs while we moved back up to our bedroom upstairs, but the kids were not interested. They were in that period where they couldn't be more than five feet away from me at any given time. When I thought they were busy and distracted I would quietly leave the room to accomplish some task elsewhere in the house, and within 30 seconds they'd be next to me. The thought of us sleeping more than a few yards away did not sit well at all.

While Liz and Randy did like the idea of sleeping farther away from us, the Cape Cod real estate market had different ideas and they too did not move as planned.

In *Animal, Vegetable, Miracle*, Barbara Kingsolver writes "[potatoes] have a built-in rest period that is calendar-neutral, and until it's over the tubers won't sprout, period." Once we settled into our new living arrangements, we hit a "built-in rest period" at the Towers. Like the potatoes, my kids knew when it was time to sprout and there was not a dang thing we could do to shift that schedule. Liz and Randy stuck around long enough to find property and build their own dream house, which was finished approximately five seconds before the kids were ready for their own rooms. People stay close during the time they need to stay close, and then they inexplicably grow/change/evolve and act like it's always been that way. It's all part of one great clock-work whole. The flowers do bloom. The tubers get their wake-up call. Everyone gets transplanted at the right time.

Years later we were ready to tear things apart again and finally replaced the kitchen. Things friends actually said when they came to our house:

"I love your kitchen! It's totally incongruous."

"It's really nice in here. It's not like a frat house anymore."

We may need friends with filters. Or I may need to stop hearing criticism where none is meant (or even if it is). I used to grab the vacuum and pretend I was in the middle of a giant cleaning spree when people showed up unexpectedly at the house. I've taken it one step farther and now cover up doorways to other parts of the house with plastic. When I see a car approaching, I grab plastic and tape, block off anything I don't want someone to see, and then track some construction dust around for good measure. People are incredibly empathetic when it looks like you're renovating. Refrigerator in your living room? No big deal. Laundry all over the kitchen counter? One would hardly imagine it otherwise.

Newsflash: We are always renovating. We're always repairing, reconsidering, and rearranging. Our homes are living organisms, with ebbs and flows and seasons and crises and moments of bright shining perfection. No wonder the laundry's on the counter.

How not to prepare for an emergency

We have "Evacuation Route" signs all down the Cape. I think they're for decoration. Not that we may not need to be evacuated some time, but if you've ever tried to get off Cape Cod on a Sunday afternoon in the summer, you can imagine what it would be like if we *all* tried to drive out of here at the same time. Fortunately at least half of us have boats in our yards, so our evacuation plan is to climb aboard and wait for the route to come to us.

I planned ahead for the latest hurricane by doing things like eating all the cookies in the house in case I have to sleep through winter. I also looked up important information in case we lose our connection to the civilized world (i.e. internet). I googled "how to wash your clothes with a rock in a pond" and then switched to "how to make clothes out of a trash bag so you can do laundry with a Swiffer."

Whenever a hurricane is on its way, we move all the stuff we don't want out into the yard, and bring in all the stuff we do want. We also wash all the laundry and the dishes – which I hear people do when there's not a hurricane coming but I can't imagine why.

Last month there was a hurricane on the way so I picked the half-ripe tomatoes and prayed for the five billion green ones to stay put. Firefly pointed out that all the weeds in our garden acted as packing material and wasn't I smart to leave them all over the place?

I filled plastic jugs with water and stuck them in the freezer. We ate Hurricane Preparedness meals for days - depleting the contents of our freezer until all that was left was the stuff we don't like anyway. I bought non-perishable-non-cookables so we could eat peanut butter and jelly for three weeks if necessary. I planned meals around what we could heat on the wood stove. I baked some tomato tarts in advance. I stashed bottles of water, although we have town water so this was only so I'd feel like part of the In Crowd while panic shopping.

And then we waited. The wind picked up and, since the rain held off, I took the dog for a walk. It was weirdly quiet (aside from the wind), and marvelous. Summers in a beach town are pretty hectic, so in a way it felt like Hurricane Jezebel was the cleaning lady coming to vacuum up the debris. I suppose a vacuuming cleaning lady would be more of a tornado, so Jezebel had a leaf blower instead. It's good to have someone or something come through with a leaf blower from time to time. I could almost feel the tension blowing out of our town. I wanted to stay out in it, but heard the gigantic crack of a branch and ran screaming for home.

The power went out at 5:15 p.m. on Sunday. By 5:30, we were seated at a restaurant ordering dinner by generator light. That's why you buy non-perishables – so when you don't eat them, they don't go bad.

The next morning, Firefly opened the fridge and the light was so bright it looked like she had interrupted an alien abduction. Both kids were psyched because first everything was dark and then, just as they were done getting ready for school by flashlight, the house went into Demonic Possession Mode. They'd flip a switch in one room, and a light would come on in another. It was awesome. I could barely get them out the door.

Chris said the ground opened, which is what it felt like. Most of the lights were out and the house smelled like melted appliances. The ground opened, and in we fell. He said that during the storm the ground wire went down, so electricity was coming into the house at 220. Judging from the smell, that's not a good thing.

Meanwhile, my mother-in-law doesn't remember things like she used to so we went over what happened a million times every 15 minutes. Note: There is something uniquely horrible about not knowing what's going on and having to tell someone the specifics of what you don't know, repeatedly.

We started with the long story, and then moved to the abbreviated version:

"There's no power."

"Is someone going to make me some toast?"

"Not right now. The power is out."

"Oh."

(pause) "Is someone going to make me some toast?"

I think if we had stabbed a piece of bread with a fork and then stuck the end of the fork in an outlet, it might have worked. But the power company deemed it dangerous and advised us to throw the main breaker until they could send a crew.

[Long pause in which we wait for aforementioned crew and then give up, going to bed at 9 because what else are we supposed to do? There's no internet and I am all caught up on my counted cross stitch by candlelight.]

At 10 p.m. I woke to an authoritative knock on the door and a tall, handsome hero from our utility company in my garden. Behind him my lawn was crawling with workers in foul weather gear. You don't realize how many windows you have until you are sitting in total darkness with searchlights bouncing off every wall in your house from outside. It's like a movie. Let me just say that I really hope the people inches from my windows, scaling my walls and shining searchlights all over my lawn in the dark of night are always using their power for good, not evil.

The next morning when the neighbors asked what all the search lights were for, I told them Firefly lost her gerbil.

24

How not to take up a hobby

When I was six we moved from the East Coast to Colorado, where we pretended we were westerners and took horseback riding lessons. The first ride I went on was with Pine, a sap-colored horse that was big and slow and some kind of Zen master. I remember Pine because we spent a lot of time alone, just standing there on the trail waiting for the rest of the riding party to finish their ride. Early in each ride, Pine would stop to smell the roses and I was not capable of either kicking him (pacifist!) or shouting for help (shy!) as the rest of the group rode away, oblivious to my plight. So we stood around a lot, just being.

Pine was far more Zen than I, and I ended up going to riding lessons with a great deal of anxiety about whether or not my horse would go. My anxiety issues did not stop there. They began with getting a blanket out of the tack room and ended...never.

I was reminded of Pine when I agreed to take sailing lessons with my upstairs neighbor, Liz. I thought you had to be a Kennedy to take sailing lessons, but it turns out they'll let anyone do it. We spent two blissful months sitting indoors with a view of the cove, learning how to tie knots. I could have stopped there, but eventually they did send us out on the water. Liz and I were shuttled out to Mr. Bill, which turned out to be a boat, not the person who was going to sail us around while we gossiped.

As we watched our instructor drive away in his Boston Whaler, Liz looked at me and said "I hate the water." She could have saved her breath, because it was pretty evident by the line of sweat above her lip, her unblinking eyes, and the way she clung to the sides of the boat like a cat about to be plunged into the bath.

I, on the other hand, do not have a fear of water. I have a fear of having no idea what I'm doing, though, so I threw myself to the bottom of the boat in solidarity. Simultaneously, from our position on the bottom of the boat we heard the voice of God. He told us to untie from our mooring and get on with it. And then the voice of God came back and got in the boat with us, knowing we would just sit there while the rest of the class rode on ahead.

He coached us through getting off the mooring. And then? And then we were sailing. It was almost like flying. Once upright, Liz did an admirable job steering while I flapped around up front. We went back and forth between those buoys, adding some decorative loop-de-loops that were not necessarily intentional. It was very fun and we wished our husbands had been there, standing slack-jawed on the dock in total awe of our sailing prowess.

And then we were glad they weren't, because it was time to get back to the mooring and while it made sense on a dry-erase board, it was completely impossible in practice. We approached the mooring in what can only be called a circular path. For reasons we have yet to understand, we can only turn the boat counter-clockwise. Which is not a nautical term. So we sailed in counter-clockwise circles, getting closer and closer to the mooring, until finally the voice of God came by and coached us in. And when that failed, he nudged us in. And then everyone involved went to the bar. We are the reason sailing clubs have bars, by the way.

We rolled up our sails, high-fived, and pinky-swore that no matter what happened, we would still be friends. We also decided that Pine had the right idea and we would be perfectly fine hanging out on the mooring for the afternoon. We're pretty Zen when it comes to sailing.

How not to host guests

Since I am not terribly social, the primary reason I plan parties at my house is so it occasionally gets clean. Cleaning around here involves several bags going to recycling and the swap shop. It's important to do this kind of clearing right before you entertain, because then you have all this lovely space and openness in your home which nature will abhor and fill within 24 hours. The window of clean is small, my friends.

But for that brief moment, your house is clean and people tell you how lovely it is and think you live like that all the time – until that one friend walks in and says *"oh my God what did you do to your house? Where are the piles? You had furniture under there?!?"*

Completely off-topic: I would love to see a version of Dwell Magazine where the interior photos are taken without notice.

Relatedly off-topic: Some day I will call all my friends and tell them a magazine is coming to do a photo shoot at our house and will they please please please come help us get ready. We need the driveway repaved, the bathroom ceiling painted and the guest room gutted. Thanks! Love you!

The Annual Trout Towers Christmas Sing is something I tried to pawn off on someone else for years. I had grown up going to a carol sing hosted by a family I babysat for in my little mountain town and it was one of my most favorite things ever. It was filled with people, music, and cookies, and ended with singing "Let There Be Peace on Earth" by candlelight. I looked forward to it every year. When I moved east, I hoped someone would would carry on the tradition and invite me. I nonchalantly mentioned it whenever I met someone with a living room large enough to fit a table of cookies, but no one picked up on it. Finally, I invited a few friends over to sing with me and the Annual Trout Towers Christmas Sing was born.

Taking a page from my book of party tips, a week before the Christmas Sing, Chris decided to tackle the kitchen floor and pulled up the linoleum. By "pulled up" I mean "lifted effortlessly." It was just lying there, except for the places where it was curling and cracking. It was awesome. Still, less than a week before a party? The man has a sense of adventure, that's for sure.

Once we decided against urethaning one dollar bills to our floor, I googled "kitchen subfloor" and came up with some beautifully painted floors. The hive mind of the internet is an excellent resource when it comes to panicking before a party. Pinterest, on the other hand, is the fast track to a nervous breakdown.

The paint guru at our local hardware store matched the glaze on a favorite dish for us – which I think means we can now eat off the floor for real. Chris put down a coat of the paint and we all gazed in rapt amazement as the nasty plywood disappeared. Once the paint was dry, Chris put on a coat of urethane, and we watched in amazement as ghastly brown streaks appeared. It turns out you're supposed to use primer if you are painting on a difficult substrate. I just learned the word "substrate" and am delighted to use it in a sentence. It is really the whole reason I'm mentioning this at all. A friend of ours was doing the same thing and it happened to them, too. Which made us feel better. Streaky floors love company.

Right! Company! Company is coming! Floor is streaking! Gah! We (Chris) repainted the floor (hahahaha! paint is roughly $900/gallon!) post haste. And then it was beautiful again. But we figured part of the problem may have been the speed with which we (Chris) put on the urethane. So we threw the floor to the wolves and left it just painted for the party. We only know it was dry because there were no paint footprints tracked through the house.

I have to admit I hate throwing parties. They always seem like a good idea until they're about to happen. If there is a hell and I end up there, it will be the two hours before a party starts. Once it starts, however, all is well. People arrive and I realize there is no connection between the quality of our floor and the quality of our friends.

Or as Emerson said, "The ornament of a house is the friends who frequent it."

How not to perform in public

Once I helped out a friend who had to leave town not completely unexpectedly. I should mention that there was no law enforcement involved in his decision to leave town – which is a refreshing change. I took over for him as house manager at a children's theater. It seemed pretty straightforward.

Still, I had a moment when all I could picture was unhappy patrons with no place to sit, strangely well-equipped with torches and pitch forks. You'd think if you're prepared enough to pack a torch and pitchfork, you could manage to fit a folding chair in there somewhere. But whatever.

The first night went off relatively hitchless; except my friend forgot to mention there was public speaking involved. In his defense, my idea of public speaking includes "may I help you find your seat?"

My daughter said "you'll be great! Come on, you're a writer." Which is precisely why I would not be great. Just because you're good with words in a public forum doesn't mean you can make them come out of your face at an appropriate time or in an appropriate order. In fact, it seems the opposite is often true. But I've been hammering into her that she can do anything she puts her mind to. I've been encouraging her to be fearless. It was time to put up or shut up.

The first time I addressed the audience it was a no-brainer. Ten minutes before curtain, I was supposed to tell everyone to go use the bathroom. I tell people all day long to go use the bathroom. The second one was trickier. It's that "turn off your cell phones," "no pictures or Sleeping Beauty will go blind and fall off the stage and die before the evil fairy has a chance to curse her," "stay out of the aisles or you'll be gored by a prince who's a little sword-happy" speech.

That's a lie about Sleeping Beauty falling off the stage before the evil fairy curses her. At that point she is only a baby and has a Cabbage Patch body double covering for her. Everyone knows Cabbage Patch body doubles adore flash photography.

Anyway. The intro music fades and I step onto the stage. House lights go down. Stage lights go up. All eyes are on me. Everyone is listening to what I am about to say.

And I have an epiphany. It is this:

We all need lighting and sound designers. Can you imagine if every time you got ready to say something like "go find your shoes," or "I need that report by morning" all the lights went off except the one that was on you? And if there was the kind of music swelling in the background that foreshadowed exactly how it was going to go down if the request was not met? You would never be ignored again.

I used to think I'd get a personal assistant and a sous chef if I won the lottery, but now I'm leaning toward a run crew. They make you disappear when you want to disappear. They put the focus on you when you need people to pay attention. They fix your broken zippers and make sure you are where you are supposed to be. Can you imagine? Just having someone tell me when it's time to get dressed would be huge. If that happened, the Peapod delivery guy might agree to start coming to our house again.

I have to tell people about the flash photography and death-by-goring again tonight, but I think I'll be okay. I can do anything I put my mind to. I am fearless.

And the crew's got my back.

How not to live sustainably

It's our fault that the planet is overheating. The ironic thing? It's our fault because we tried to do the right thing.

When we renovated, we left our hall bathroom with an orange extension cord running through the hall to power a small lamp with a naked bulb. Months later, in a burst of optimistic productivity, Chris tackled the lighting situation. He hooked up the light fixtures and dashed off for a new switch because he didn't like the old one. The old one was in the hall and I think that Chris, the youngest of three, doesn't trust having the light switch where other people can get to it. That's just my opinion and since it's become abundantly more clear with every passing day that Chris and I do not think alike *at all*, it's probably something else. Maybe it disturbs the air flow in the hall.

I need to take a moment right here and tell you a little about the man I love. If there is a simple way to do something, Chris will complicate it. The new way will be genius, but unwieldy. For example, when we got married I gave away my stereo because I figured since I was marrying a sound engineer I didn't need it. I never did learn how to play my CDs through his sound board, no matter how easy he said it was. He is super smart and full of ideas that start with "this might be crazy but...."

So instead of a light switch, Chris came back with a motion sensor. You walk in the bathroom and it turns on. When you leave, it notices you are no longer fussing about and turns off. Easy peasy.

Problems, in no particular order:

1. Sketch was too short to activate the sensor.
2. The light had zero patience with us and turned itself off in about 10 seconds.

Okay, that's pretty much all I've got. I would mostly just elaborate if I kept going. For instance, I would tell you how if Sketch got the light to go on (by jumping up and down and waving the bathmat), the light would then go back off just as he was balanced on his tippy toes and trying to aim. The sensor scored major points for comedic timing.

In no time flat, we learned to use the override option, turning the light on at the switch manually and then leaving it on. For days. That light was on longer than any other light in our house.

Our hearts are in the right place, though. This is new for me, as I was not raised to have a heart in the right place. I can't speak for Chris (although I often do), but I was raised on opera and skiing and cake. We like music festivals that are not at a county fair. We shop at Whole Foods because it looks and sounds delicious. We buy organic food because that aisle is generally less crowded. We have smaller cars because they are easier to park and less likely to draw the attention of someone who needs help moving. We do not buy them because they use less gas, although that's really paying off.

Nevertheless, we have chickens, a not-completely-laughable vegetable garden, a shelf full of home-canned chutney, and an energy efficient light that never goes off. I don't know who we are anymore.

It started with the chickens. We got them because we have friends who had them and they seemed no more prepared to parent chickens than we were, which somehow made it a good idea. It turned out to be one of our better decisions because they're cute and fluffy and seem to like me. Perhaps even more importantly they make this whole place make sense. Now, people drive up to the house and say "what the..... oh! they have chickens!" Besides, they cut my grocery bill in, like, *half*. Okay not half. They may actually have doubled my grocery bill but that is not the point here.

When we first thought about getting chickens we were concerned about the coyotes across the street. A huge, thriving, colony of coyotes. So we built Fort McChicken, a luxury compound with gated entrance and enhanced security features (read: old baby monitor). Fort McChicken was not the plan when I first introduced the idea. I found plans for very simple, build-in-a-weekend coops on the internet, as well as several magazine articles on starting a small flock. We were essentially looking at a dog house with nesting boxes. Because coops were so easy to build, we put the cart before the horse, or the chicken before the egg, and set out to find us some chicks.

We had hoped to get them from an elementary school class that was hatching chickens because we liked the idea of them coming from an academic environment. We also didn't have any idea where else to get them. I have always equated livestock with large farming equipment, but it turns out two children can walk into a feed and grain store and buy five baby chicks as a Mother's Day gift, no questions asked.

We kept the chicks in a box in our living room and named them all after songs: Lola, Prudence, Sweet Jane, Gloria, and Mustang Sally. The chickens are supposed to stay inside until they get real feathers, but weeks later when those feathers came in there was still no coop for them to move into. So they stayed, and grew. And grew. They grew so much that we needed to expand their accommodations in our living room. So I went to the home improvement store in town in hopes of scoring an appliance box.

All they had was a refrigerator box, which definitely was not fitting in our little car. I called a few large-vehicled friends, but no one was available. It was getting late and I didn't want to seem ungrateful and just leave the box there, so I told them I'd go ahead and carry it home. They looked at me in that way I am becoming accustomed to.

"It's a small town – I'll probably see someone I know with a truck in the parking lot," I told them, and headed off with the refrigerator box balanced on my head. Firefly maneuvered the stroller because of course I had the kids with me. Everything's easier with a couple toddlers in tow.

There was no one in the parking lot. Rather, there were a lot of people in the parking lot, but no one who was willing to make eye contact. I thought *surely there will be someone we know driving past*. It really is a small town and you can't go anywhere without seeing someone you know – unless you're carrying a refrigerator box on your head.

The chickens grew more. We still had no coop, so we went back to the home improvement store and got another box – this time a nice conveniently-sized washing machine box. We were like ants, traversing town with empty appliance boxes on our backs for the sake of building the chickens a Habitrail in our living room. By the time the coop was ready it was July 4th weekend and the chickens were the size of dachshunds.

What is this world in which you can buy live baby chickens in your not terribly rural tourist town and house them in your living room for three months? When did micro-farming become the new knitting?

When I lived in Boulder I loved shopping at a store called Alfalfas. There were two Alfalfas markets within walking distance – the one on The Hill and the one on the Pearl Street Mall.

The one on The Hill was good if you weren't raised by flower children and don't know your amaranth from your umeboshi. The one on Pearl Street had a spider-plant-in-hemp-macrame kind of vibe to it, where on The Hill you could actually recognize some things. When I went to the one on Pearl Street I always felt out of my depth.

There was this awkward conjunction of not knowing what things were, and the fear of asking. Inevitably I bought sesame sticks.

Much of what they sold on Pearl Street is common now: bulgur, flax, groats, adzuki beans, seitan, etc. We know what they are now because of Alfalfas on The Hill and others like it (the one I shopped at in Denver is now a Whole Foods, to give you an idea of what it was like). They took Groat Bake and made it look like a deli special instead of penance.

We got our first chickens at the feed and grain store equivalent of the Pearl Street Alfalfas. I felt like I should know what I needed – there are lives at stake, for crying out loud – but had no idea what anything was. I asked questions and found the things I needed, but I always felt like an outsider. I don't know why. We are incredible chicken farmers.

Like the time I returned home to see that a spaceship had landed in our yard. Chris looked pleased at the spaceship, so I said "uh, wow honey. Is that a new chicken coop?" He nodded.

"What does it look like?" he asked.

"A really big spin-art thing?"

"No."

"A septic tank?"

"No. Someplace we've been."

I am sure lots of people who shop at the feed and grain store house their chickens in a scale model of the Smithsonian's Hirshhorn Museum. Seeking closure, I went to our local hardware store to get a scale tensegrity Needle Tower to go in the sculpture garden of our new coop and ran into some friends. They were gathering leaves from a particular tree to feed to their silkworms.

I feel so pedestrian.

How not to find your way home

We have the kind of house that spiders look at and, clasping their foremost hands together, say "oh honey, it's perfect!" And then they eat their mates.

Our predecessors on this spit of land built houses that looked like fish. Scales and all. It's like we collectively decided we had displeased God and took up residence in the belly of giant fish.

Have you lived where you live long enough to have stopped seeing it? Sometimes I think back and remember how this town looked to me when I first moved here. The first cottage I rented was on a pond. It was a summer rental, and tiny, tiny, tiny except for the enclosed porch, which was my bedroom. My roommate's room had a window that opened into my room. There was another bed in the hall and we intended to get a third roommate, but she never showed up. The kitchen was under the eaves and you had to duck to get into the bathroom. The water was so full of iron I got rust stains on my white waitressing shirts. At night I would come home from work and go swimming in the pond. It was just a bunch of frogs and me.

I thought everyone lived on the water. My next cottage was on marshland, which I mistook for swamp. I didn't appreciate it at first but did spend those years with a bird book on my night table. Red winged blackbirds are still some of my favorites. And the first time I saw a goldfinch I thought someone's pet canary had escaped because I am not from here and we are not allowed to have delicate, pretty things where I come from. I also remember seeing a vending machine that looked like it would have drinks in it but was actually dispensing worms.

Sometimes when I go to The Big City (pop. 48,000) I come back on the side roads instead of taking the highway. There are stone walls and cottage gardens, little stores, village centers, hundred year old homes, a horse pasture, and bay views. The cherry trees are glorious. Sometimes if the wind is right you can smell the ocean from the middle of town. You don't just smell it, you can feel it on your skin – a tingly saltiness, a thickness to the air.

I guess it's the same as with any other crush. Part of the infatuation is based on what we actually know of the person/place/thing, but a good deal of it is the fiction we create around them. As we become acquainted, the reality may turn out to be better than the fiction – even if it's a little less exotic than we first thought. Eventually we become the exotic ones for those just starting to create their own fiction. If they only knew.

Recently Chris and I discovered that we don't live where we think we live. You see, Chris had ordered a computer for a client and needed it the next day. He had it overnighted, but it didn't show up so he called UPS who told us we don't exist. We don't exist because our mailbox number is different from our house number. One of those numbers was made up by my mother-in-law, because she wanted her own address. It's worked for years and no one's ever questioned it – until the substitute UPS driver couldn't find our house.

But all was not lost, including the package. It turns out our neighbor down the street and around the corner works at UPS and heard our name and address being tossed around. She brought the package on her way home and had no trouble with the misleading house number – because we live in the Finley's old house and that's enough for most people in town. I explained about the house number thing and she said "aw, that's nothing. We have people tell us, 'the house number is under the wisteria' or 'our street is really a driveway but we named it.'"

The last time I used navigation to find my way somewhere around here I was glad I looked at the map instead of just printing out the directions. There were at least 4 turns that had no street signs. None. Or the signs were there but all the letters had fallen off. It seems a very New England thing to do: "If you can't find my house, you're not invited."

Unless you're a package we've ordered, on which our continued employment depends. As I stood in my driveway chatting with our down the street and around the corner neighbor, I realized with horror that I sometimes buy plants from her family and she was standing with a full view of our garden. Thankfully it was evening. Everything looks better in the evening, and from the outside.

When Chris and I got married we had a mini-moon and went to the North Shore (north of Boston yet still in Massachusetts). Our first destination was Rockport, where we drove and walked and explored and decided important things about our new marriage such as where to stay and what to have for dinner. At one point we had a beautiful view of the harbor at twilight. There was a restaurant right on the water and it looked simply magical – what with all those people sitting in the twinkly lights having dinner in this beautiful spot. We envied them and decided to have dinner there.

We got a table by the window and now – *voilà!* – we were those people. And that's when we noticed that if you are sitting in the twinkly lights you can't actually see the twinkly lights. In fact, all we could see from the window was darkness. They could at least have floated some candles in the harbor for us, no?

Fortunately this was not a metaphor for our marriage. Or maybe it was. Because since there was nothing but darkness outside, we turned our attention to the menu in front of us. And then because we are poor planners and because the thrill of the hunt is half the adventure, we started looking for a place to stay.

We found a place that was also right on the water. We fell asleep to the sound of waves on the shore. When we woke up we watched lobstermen check their traps. It was every bit as beautiful and perfect as we thought it would be. And we found it because we drove by and noticed the lights reflected in the water.

Sometimes I drive up to our house in the evening when all the lights are on inside and I think "now there's a place I'd like to be." In partial darkness you don't see the unfinished projects, and the lights look like a big Welcome sign. Sometimes when I get bogged down and frustrated I step outside and look back at my home from a quieter perspective. And then I hear my dad's voice in my head and I run inside to turn off lights and make sure the windows are closed so we're not heating/lighting/air conditioning the neighborhood for crying out loud.

Sometimes I try to make my house look normal inside and out, especially when people are coming over. Okay, exclusively when people are coming over because who really cares otherwise? When the kids were little this happened a lot because of all the playdates. They were invited to friends' houses and of course eventually we had to reciprocate. If you doubt the existence of a spreadsheet tally of playdate equity, that may explain the hostility you sometimes encounter at the grocery store.

Playdates were easy until the kids made friends who hadn't been personally selected by me, at which point people I had never met started coming over. While the kids play, I essentially run interference between the visiting adult and everything about my life I don't want them to see. On one occasion, I ran out to ensure guests came to the door that opens and not the door where we keep everything that's going to the dump, and was intercepted in the driveway by Sketch. He was wearing nothing, *nothing*, but a pair of ruby slippers he had borrowed from Firefly. I don't know why I bother. During the course of the day all our deep dark secrets trotted out and said hello. No, I don't mean the friends who came by for various reasons. I mean the little stories and assorted oddities which comprise our home. Why, for instance, we have lead rods in our yard. Why we have a wood stove in our driveway. Why we have a sandbox with no sand despite living at the beach.

While we were outside the two littlest ones decided it was fun to go into the house through the side door, cut through the kitchen and then come out through the screen door. I don't mean "through the screen door" in the usual sense of opening and closing it. I mean that they were crawling through a massive hole in what used to be the screen. And then they ran to the side door and did it again. And again – in case no one had noticed.

Sometimes it's good when people come by the house and notice something is broken. Once when Chris was recording a band here the guitar player noticed that our toilet wasn't working properly. He was in the process of tearing down a house and suggested salvaging a toilet and bringing it over for us to install. "It's so easy," he told me. "Have you ever put in a toilet?" I am not sure how I have lived this long and not put in a toilet.

True to his word, the loudest guitar player in the world brought a toilet over the next day. It's a low-flush toilet, which was a gigantic improvement over our old, continual flush model. And we didn't have to spend money on it, which is good because in the 17 pages that comprise my latest Christmas list you will not find "new toilet."

This whole salvaging thing is new to me. Over the years we've made use of many salvaged things – our back door, the upstairs fridge, some cupboards and now this. It's the way things are done around here. And by "here" I mean Cape Cod. And by Cape Cod I mean the Lower/Outer Cape. When they took down the old Uncle Tim's Bridge in Wellfleet, all the lumber was hauled off by various people to use on various projects. I heard they didn't need to take much of anything to the dump. It's the same spirit that drove people to the beaches in the wee hours of the morning to scavenge valuables washed up on shore after a shipwreck. We've just stopped waving our lanterns on moonless nights, trying to get the ships to wreck.

Everything has a use. Have you ever noticed how much stuff there is in Chinese restaurants? Bamboo and chimes and flutes and fans and auspicious this and that. It must be working because the Chinese restaurant that made me think about all this has been in town for at least 20 years. That's pretty impressive considering how hard we are on restaurants around here. They usually leave town in tears after a year or two.

I see these decorations/good luck symbols, and wonder if we'd do well with some sprigs of bamboo at our house. Maybe a red door. Or a water feature that's not in a hamster cage. There are so many things we could do to luck the place up. But then, what would people think? Would they think we felt we were somehow lacking? Would they look at our carefully arranged whatnots and conclude that we have skeletons in our Helpful People closet? That our bread is apt to mold? That our mice are anemic?

Same goes for those stone bracelets that look like rosary beads. You know the ones? They're made of rose quartz or amethyst or hematite or something else that's good for whatever your issue may be. I pick them up, run them through my fingers and wonder what they're for. Then I imagine a total stranger pointing to it on my wrist and saying something like "can't keep a boyfriend, eh?" I can totally see myself yelling at an unsuspecting passerby: "I can keep a boyfriend just fine, thank you!" which I would then have to explain to my husband.

I was not raised in a tradition rich in auspicious signs and wonders. However, I have created my own tradition of never telling anyone what I'm afraid of. Did you see *Witches of Eastwick*? It's a bad idea to answer the question "what are you afraid of" honestly. I think the answer is in finding enigmatic cures that aren't part of the usual repertoire. We like to keep people guessing. Our cures come and go because everything comes and goes so we have to keep changing our dosage. At any given time our cures may include:

Baby chicks in the living room = hope

Piles of spring clothes on the way into the kids' drawers = growth

Piles of discarded clothes on the way to Good Will = gratitude

Half-eaten apple crisp in kitchen = happiness

Extra family members = community

Dining room floor covered with art supplies = activity

There are more, but they're secret. All I will tell you is that they make it difficult to walk through the living room without tripping. Others are filling the chairs and a couple are stashed on top of the fridge. They all have meaning, if you give me a minute to think about it.

And you thought we didn't have all this stuff strewn about on purpose.

How not to put off your eye exam

It has come to my attention that I can't see as well as I once could. This is most apparent when someone presents a splinter to be removed. I cannot see the splinter and estimated guesses as to its whereabouts are under-appreciated.

After a period of fretting and hand-wringing and worst case scenario-izing, I made an eye appointment. I don't know why I put it off. Eye appointments are fabulous. You should really make them more than every 20 years. The chair is comfy and they even give you a place to rest your chin. All chairs should come with foot and chin rests. Once you are nice and comfortable, they ask you to do things that are much less repulsive than the other things you have to do in the course of a day. You read letters, top to bottom, until you get to the line of hieroglyphs. The hieroglyphs are there to trick you. Then they ask you questions. I get asked questions all day long but I don't know the answers to those questions. Those are questions like "why are we so far over budget?" and "who totaled the company car?" The optometrist asks questions like "which one's clearer? A or B?"

I like questions I know the answers to. And if I get them wrong, who will know? I could tell I was getting them right because the more I answered, the better I could see. It was like magic! Toward the end, the letters looked like they had been cut with a scalpel from black construction paper.

But that's not the interesting part. After the "exactly how blind are you" part of the exam, they start looking at the eyeball proper. They put drops in your eyes and after dropping the drops they say "that's yellow highlighter" and you're all "hahahahaha! that's funny! As if you would actually draw on my eye with a yellow highlighter!" and you wipe a little laugh-tear from your eye with a tissue and it looks like a bug got squashed in your eye because the tissue is bright, bright, bug-gut yellow and it turns out they did actually put yellow highlighter in your eye.

Just as you are deciding never to trust them again, they put another drop in your eyes and tell you they are testing the pressure. The drops will make your eyes feel like they are wrapped in double stick tape. Finally, they put drops in your eyes to dilate your pupils, and send you to the waiting room to look at magazines but not read them because you have yellow highlighter and double stick tape in your eyes. When they get you back in the chair, they tell you they're going to look inside your eye with a bright light. What they don't tell you is that they are looking inside your eye for ants which they then set on fire with the light and a magnifying glass. It's the only possible explanation for someone to point a light that bright at you. Also, I know that's what they're doing because after they do it, all you can see is exploding ant fireballs.

And then they tell you you need glasses, which you pick out while still under the influence of exploding ant fireballs.

Which explains a lot.

How not to exercise

One time I downloaded a yoga podcast. It was a Kundalini Yoga sequence, which I'd never done before. Oh I've done the breathing with sharp exhalation that makes you wish you had gone for a tissue before class, but I've never done the lying down on the floor with arms over head and sit up to forward bend 21 times. There was also a pilates-esque move which looked a bit like a crunch but was way, way worse. I know all about Pilates because I have a book on Pilates right over there on the shelf and I saw something like this on the cover.

I also subscribed to *Coffee Break Spanish*, which I'll listen to when I'm driving around wishing I were smarter. In fact, I may just listen to both podcasts in the car. That way I can be conversant in Spanish and Yoga. And really, I just want the ability to talk about things with some element of conviction. I can say "oh, in this morning's yoga podcast the warm-up was a *chaturanga* to headstand sequence. Twenty-one times!" No one needs to know that I was driving up to the Dunkin' Donuts window while it was happening.

Someone recently posted one of those "ask your kids these adorable questions about you" things and of course I fell for it. Let me tell you, there are reasons people warn you not to take these quizzes. No, it did not steal my birthdate, blood type and mother's maiden name. It did something far worse.

It all started a few months ago with the world's best parenting trick. Seriously. I am a genius. You're going to wish you had thought of it.

Last fall my son's soccer coach suggested he get extra running in so he wouldn't have to stop periodically and look for four leaf clovers. He gets that from me. I have never been a runner, despite frequent attempts. I am a wheezing, gasping, sweaty mess by the end of the driveway. I stop at the end of the driveway because no one in the actual outside world needs to see that.

First I had Sketch run around the block, but the block's not very far and he got bored. Driving alongside him worked until they kicked me off the bike path. And then I remembered Couch to 5k. With Couch to 5k you start with nice long walks speckled with short bits of running. I bought the app, laced up my sneakers and hit the road with my son, where I discovered these truths:

1. A running partner whose legs are literally half as long as yours is a good thing.
2. Sixty seconds of running is hideous and nausea-inducing.
3. People see what they expect to see – and are kinder and more generous with their expectations than is reasonable.

What happened: I miraculously kept my whinging to myself with my son trotting alongside.

What people saw: A great and supportive mom, slowing it down for her boy.

I kid you not. People were practically throwing flowers.

I can't tell you how great this was. Half my problem was how embarrassed I am to plod along in public. Suddenly my snail's pace was making people's hearts swell with gratitude for this obvious evidence of kindness and good parenting.

Admiration and approval is very motivational – even if the admiration is founded on a lie. You might think that I'd respond by becoming the mom people mistook me for. That I now sport a super cute running dress and accompany him at half marathons. You'd be wrong, but only because something even better happened: I got to know my boy.

We were both out of breath most of the time – me starting with the tying of the shoes and him after the first spell of running – but I noticed that he was willing to talk while gasping for air, which distracted him from the stopwatch. So I asked him questions. Short, monosyllabic questions.

I learned what was going on in school, what he liked, what he was excited about, what projects he wanted to do, and all sorts of things I still have no idea about but are probably apps. On the trail we could talk about anything and everything.

I asked things like "what's that?" "what's it do?" and "tell me more" to keep him going. This will sound ludicrous, but I actually wanted my single-digit aged son to keep talking. I especially tried to get him on a roll when the app was about to say "Let's Run!" so I could pretend to miss the cue.

He always heard it, and we ran.

We ran for six weeks and made a lot of progress, staying with the program despite the voice in my head telling me we were going to die. And then the weather changed and I had to beg out because who knew cold air burns the lungs like freaking acid? After a couple weeks of waiting for the searing to stop, I decided I was off the hook and could give up running with a clear conscience. I had given it a good and valiant effort. Soccer season was over and so was I.

And then that stupid "ask your kids these adorable questions about you" thing happened. Months after we stopped, his answer to "What do you enjoy doing with your mom?" was still "running." For extra guilt-inducing credit, his answer to "what makes your mom happy" was "me." Remind me of this when I'm gasping for air on the next non-sub-zero day, running at a pace slightly slower than that at which you watch tv.

I don't know why he likes running with me. I am whiny, slow, and unfashionable. But I suppose it must be done. The entire town must be worried sick, wondering what happened to that darling little jogger boy and the best mom ever. If they're looking for me, I'm doing yoga in my car. In Spanish.

How not to grow a garden

When real estate agents say that gardens increase property value, they don't mean ours. Fortunately, that's not why we planted it. Nor did we plant it to heighten our esteem in the eyes of the neighbors. We planted it so we can care for something and watch it grow, and be amazed, and then eat it. We grow so the kids will know that vegetables don't come from the store – and because I'm too cheap to buy all those fresh herbs at the Farmer's Market, and too snobby to cook without them.

I would tell you what's what in my garden but I have no idea. Once I put seeds out there they are as good as dead so I discard all memorabilia promptly. That way when something lives, it's a happy surprise.

Our vegetable garden is placed so you have to walk through it to get into the house. I find this incredibly gratifying. It's like if you built shelves in your living room and moved your whole pantry there – housed in attractive containers – where you can see everything. I happen to find looking at an abundance of edibles soothing. And decorative.

We don't know the first thing about raising vegetables, which is why it was so funny the year we planted corn next to our front door. There's something iconic about cornstalks. Twelve corn plants somehow send you over the edge into Hardcore Agrarian because now you live in a cornfield. Did you know that the ears of corn grow out of the sides of the stalk, not out of the top? I was all "yes, but where's the corn?" and then I noticed some tufty bits on the side. Who knew?

If you came by our house that year and looked closely, you would have noticed that at some point during the summer our corn dyed its hair. In corn years it was in its early teens, so we shouldn't have been surprised about the pink hair. This is the sort of thing that happens to us. We try to do something normal (corn in your flower bed is normal. We read it somewhere) and everything goes all King's Road when we're not looking. Deciding to roll with it, we changed our chickens' names to Wendy O. Williams, Exene Cervenka, Nina Hagan, Lena Lovich, Patti Smith, Palmolive and Amanda Palmer. Then we had to go get more chickens because seriously, we could go on like that for ages.

People ask us about the chickens all the time. How much work they are, how many eggs we get, what on earth possessed us to get chickens – stuff like that. They think they would like to have chickens of their own to name but they don't do it because they're not in the same position we are.

I'm not 100% clear what that position is. For a long time I thought they were under the impression that we have some kind of innate agricultural leanings, which we don't. Then reality kicks in and I am forced to admit that even a cursory glance at us provides everything one needs to know about our farming skills.

What I have come to realize is that it has nothing to do with agriculture, this perception people have of us. We are not agricultural people; we are people who don't care what the neighbors think. That's what they mean by the position we're in. Or maybe they just know how awesome our neighbors are. Our neighbors are so awesome they've taken to reading Bukowski to the corn when the rest of us are sleeping. They say you should talk to your plants, and we're here to say that corn with pink hair and an attitude is delicious.

Nearly everyone knows more about gardening than we do, which is incredibly handy. For those of us who are not innately social, it's great always to have something in your pocket to talk about. If nothing whatsoever grew to maturity in our garden, it would be worth it for the social awkwardness it alleviates.

Our friend Sarah designed our vegetable garden by outlining the beds in orange spray paint so we had to do something about it. She's the one I once overheard talking to another gardener about receding flowers, making it sound as if receding was a good thing. I was confused, since I didn't know flowers even had hairlines. It turns out they had reseeded. I have things that reseed in my garden, too. Rogue cosmos and tomatoes, mostly. And lots of weeds. They're pretty good at reseeding. Some of these things she refers to as "exotic invasives." She also sometimes refers to other things as exotic invasives, such as the wrens who were imported as decoration and now are running for town council.

I like saying "exotic invasives" because it makes me sound smart. So you can imagine my delight when I looked around the grocery store one summer evening and identified 90% of the shoppers as exotic invasives. It was 5:00 p.m. on vacation rental change-over day, and the parking lot was full of out of state license plates, which I pointed out saying "exotic invasive, exotic invasive, exotic invasive. You over there? Exotic invasive."

Except in order to be truly invasive you have to stay. You have to move in, put down roots and send up little shoots who will soon need desk space at the local elementary school. Most tourists don't do that. They are simply exotic. Me? I'm invasive. I've been here since the '90s which in absolutely no way makes me a native. To be honest, I've never thought of myself as exotic before so I'd probably pick that over native anyway. Either way, here I am putting down roots and sending up shoots. Now, those little shoots are how I learn most of what I know about gardening. When she was in elementary school I had

Firefly infiltrate Garden Club so she could report her findings. She'd come home from school with "we planted garlic today" and out we ran for garlic to plant. Every garden needs a mole.

Chris says we should chop down some trees and add more vegetable plots. We are obviously in the honeymoon phase of the vegetable garden, not in the "man cannot live on snap peas alone" phase. Statements like these are likely to win him the same fate as our beets, carrots, bibb lettuce and broccoli – which, shall we say, are no longer among the living. One of these days I'll tally up all my vegetable garden expenses. I will do this if Chris threatens to make us quit our day jobs and become farmers. Perhaps we should put a fainting couch in the garden in preparation for that day. Until then, I throw the term "sustainable agriculture" around when I want some kind of fancy lobster compost.

Even in summers of unexpected bounty, I can't imagine how people live off this stuff. In the middle of winter I have visions of how I'll feed the family vegetables we've grown and we'll spend something like $4 a month on things like flour and sugar. And then summer comes and we eat lettuce, snap peas, zucchini, and about 14 leaves of spinach before it bolts.

Those snap peas are delicious, though, so we continue to water all our little plants and sing them songs. In the afternoon the three or four of us report to the vegetable patch to root around with our size-specific trowels. And maybe when we're all in the garden, looking puzzled and waving our trowels around, we are actually increasing some kind of property value.

One time a year or so ago, just after the window of burning opportunity closed, Chris took a chainsaw to nearly every living thing in our yard. I think his vision for our home includes a sweeping lawn leading up to the manor on top of the hill. His vision may or may not include peacocks. Which would be awesome. Can you train peacocks to stay inside an invisible fence? We could get them some stunning, jewel-encrusted, electrocuting collars. If we were not so reasonable, that is. Not that jewel-encrusted collars are unreasonable. But do people eat peacock eggs? Around here, form definitely follows function. Which is why we have Decorative Lawn Chickens strolling the grounds. Maybe we could take the chickens to the salon and get them tail feather extensions. A chicken with a peacock tail would be magnificent. The girls would be thrilled right out of their little chicken minds.

But this is not about Decorative Lawn Chickens and their tail extensions (which I will now patent). It is about Chris and his Burn Pile of Awesomeness. As I said, he took a chainsaw to pretty much everything. He did a fine job, except we had to administer smelling salts to Sarah when she saw he had cut the yews to stumps. Had Chris known they were yews, he could have sculpted them into peacock topiary and saved the tail extension technician a lot of time and peck wounds.

The pile Chris created from all this chainsawing was magnificent. Thirty feet across and heaped as high as he could get it, that pile sat in our yard for almost a year waiting for burn season. The peacocks would have had a fit. When that glorious first day of burn season finally came, I think I saw Chris' fire from two towns down. Chris, who has been known to haul out an old vacuum and blow it into the pile for added oxygenated speed-burning, actually hooked up the garden hose and had it ready, just in case. You know it's big when Chris takes precautions. He even moved the Upstairs Neighbor's truck. You're welcome, Randy! You still have a truck!

The cathartic aspect of burning down your own yard and/or

tending a garden is woefully under-represented. In what other areas of your life can you rip out everything that offends you, leaving it to die in the sun or go up in flames? Think how gratifying it would be to move through work, home, and your own brain, discarding everything that doesn't belong and will not bear fruit. Imagine standing back, covered in dirt, admiring the grounds where only the things you want are cultivated. I discovered the cathartic nature of gardening accidentally. In times of trouble I would answer a phone call from my sister and tell her I had time to talk but the garden desperately needed weeding. Both of these things were true, but it was I who needed weeding. I went outside to have a little privacy and not rant/panic/weep openly in front of the kids.

There were a few horrible years when our garden was notably free of weeds. This summer you could barely see the harvest for the weeds, and I couldn't be happier. Now I need to remember only to plant things I want to harvest. I know this sounds obvious, but judging from other areas of my life I'm likely to end up with a garden full of collard greens and self righteous indignation.

How not to care for aging parents

No one actually wants to hear about your Thanksgiving when they ask how it was, unless it goes completely off the rails. One year, everyone wanted to hear about our Thanksgiving.

In my mother-in-law's defense, she entered Thanksgiving all jacked down on painkillers from a recent back injury. Combined with a lethal cocktail of confusion and memory loss, the painkillers turned our already outspoken grandma into a flamethrower draped in a housecoat. Nothing was right for her. Gram hated the cheese on the relish tray. We'd hand her something to try and she'd yell at us. And then she'd complain that no one was giving her anything to eat.

My mom, on the other hand, was starting to display her own idiosyncrasies. Or rather, the idiosyncrasies that had always been pushed under the surface by a relentless sense of propriety began popping up here and there as propriety wandered off to pick flowers. Unlike Gram, Nana loved the relish tray, especially the gorgonzola which she ate off the cheese knife.

Fortunately for all of us, dinner was ready promptly.

Because of the painkillers, I offered Gram a ginger ale instead of the box of wine that probably would have fixed everything. She made a face at me, so I listed the other options. More faces ensued, ranging from "who even buys that?" to "you're actively trying to kill me, aren't you?" Finally, she had a verdict.

"I don't give a damn what you give me," she said.

That pretty much sums up dinner. Everything, from the lack of toast to the inexplicable presence of turkey, was wrong and wrathful. And that's not even getting into the national debate over jellied versus whole berry cranberry sauce.

Nana watched all this with horror. Not that she liked all the choices either, but by golly it's Thanksgiving and you are honor-bound to at least appear thankful. Even though the sniping was never directed toward her, Nana finally could not take it and began praying loudly at the dinner table. We're not talking grace here. We're talking the-Pope-should-take-notes stream of consciousness prayer.

Did I mention there were guests? There were guests. Guests who had to excuse themselves from the table to live tweet the event. I know this because I ran into one on her way out of the bathroom, phone in hand, as I was heading in to send World's Worst Thanksgiving texts to my sister.

In actuality, it wasn't the World's Worst Thanksgiving by a long shot. We had plenty of food, a roof over our heads and – in some form or another – each other. I worried about the kids and long term emotional scarring, but the kids were only worried about getting the right kind of pie. It turns out you can't ruin Thanksgiving for anyone but yourself. You can send the appearance up in flames, but you can't touch the real thing.

This is true of Gram, too. While situations including pain, memory loss, and mind-altering meds made things difficult for her, she was quite often herself. Despite aggressively grumpy appearances, we had much to be grateful for.

For a little while we had both grandmothers living with us, which brought our total at the time to two grandmothers, two friends, two children, six chickens, three cats, a quantity of mice, and us. It was kind of awesome.

How, you ask, can it be kind of awesome? Because Chris loves my mom more than he loves me. Or perhaps he is more deeply shamed by her. At any rate, he scampered out and bought screens for our windows and suddenly as of the twentieth of August in the hottest summer known to humankind, our windows opened.

Every night when I tuck the kids in bed I ask them what they are grateful for because I am selfish and like to hear them rehearse all the marvelous things I've done for them during the day. Topping their hit parade at this time was "I'm grateful Nana is here."

Since there was no room for her in the chicken coop, despite the pleasant summer weather, we had to give Nana our bedroom. I set up a little reading nook for her in the corner of the bedroom, which I can't believe I hadn't thought of before since hiding in the corner behind a book is completely my MO. In the meantime we slept in the living room, which is very much like going on vacation thanks to that where-am-I-what-day-is-it-which-way-is-the-bathroom feeling you get when you wake up elsewhere. It takes so very little.

Before long she moved back home and we had to come back from our vacation/exile. Not long after that, we realized we needed to find her a new place to live. We couldn't imagine her in a retirement home, but we also couldn't keep driving an hour to deliver her groceries and make sure the stove had been turned off. After a summer of coercion, manipulation, and negotiation we convinced her to move into the sweetest place imaginable, where we got to hang out with her and use the eight slice toaster in the community dining hall willy-nilly. It was completely great right up until she got kicked out.

It wasn't us who got her kicked out. No one told me I'd have to find more than one place for my mom to live. I thought my work was done once I got her out of her beautiful and much loved home and into an equally beautiful place where she didn't have to cook or drive. However, the day eventually came when they were no longer able to meet her needs.

At one point in the kicking out process, my sister and I were asked to join a conference call about mom's options (or lack thereof). I remember it distinctly because I took the call sitting in my car outside of Town Hall in Provincetown. When the home's director was finished giving us the reasons it wasn't working, and the dire timeline we were under, I stayed on the line with my sister and told her where I was, because having a "5 Lesbians Eating a Quiche" banner hanging over your head while drag queens walk by make bad news more colorful if not more palatable.

I had a list of Phase Two places in mind. Some of them were lovely, while others were acceptable only because they weren't That Place – the one that is fine for people who are crazy or whose kids obviously don't love them. I put her name on waiting lists, took tours, did research, and then I moved her into That Place because the universe found giving me no alternative hilarious.

When it was time for her to move, That Place was exactly what she needed. It kept her safe and provided for needs I hadn't realized she had. They even made their own bread because they discovered the smell of baking bread was something the residents dearly missed. It was perfect for her until I had to move her again – this time into Hell No. It's funny how fast the phrase "I will never..." comes around to bite you.

By the time she moved to Hell No I had been called by hospital staff on two occasions to say my goodbyes because they were sure it was time and had never met my mom so didn't know better. Nursing staff is so incredibly nice when you are saying your goodbyes, but I am here to tell you that when your loved one rouses herself and reenters consciousness with a loud and fervent prayer, *you are dead to them*. One minute they're bringing you clementines, and the next you can't get so much as a box of tissues.

I moved mom into Hell No at the same time I was going for a CT Scan, MRI, and echocardiogram of my own. I remember stopping to pick up lunch at a market between the hospital and Hell No, and eating an entire bucket of brownie bites on my way to fill out the paperwork necessary to get my mom moved in. If you woke up one day and had no feelings whatsoever, it's because I ate them.

In my defense, it had been a long haul. During the Days of Peace, when mom was safely moved to the retirement home of our dreams and prayers, Gram was on hospice at the house.

I thought hospice was like putting your name in for a table at a restaurant. Technically hospice is when you have six months or less, but the hostess really has no idea when your name will come up, if it comes up at all. It is either the longest six months or the shortest six months of your life, depending on your situation.

Up until the time I lived through it myself, I was under the impression that hospice was a place of comfort and refuge. I envisioned it as a sanctuary, where all one's needs were met by a kindly medieval monk. In my mind hospice smells nice, is well lit, and sounds like Enya.

I thought people spent all their time with people in hospice because a) of course you want to be with them and b) who wouldn't want to hang out drinking twig tea with a medieval monk? But it turns out that you are required to stay with your loved one even if you don't like Enya or the smell of crisp, line-dried sheets because they cannot be alone and help only comes for an hour a day. Which immediately makes you want to leave.

Or at least that's how I felt. Gram had turned into a caricature of a grumpy old woman. As Chris said to the kids one morning, "Gram used to be really nice. She used to be just like mama."

You should have seen the look on Sketch's face when he said that. He looked at me, and the light dawned

"Oh no," he said

I did not want to turn into a grumpy old woman earlier than necessary, so I busied myself with important soul-saving tasks like online shopping. Which is how we ended up with the tent.

I saw it on Amazon and immediately knew we had to have it. Just think of the possibilities. We could go camping! We could use it as a guest room! We could hide our heads in the sand in privacy! I told everyone it was for the kids, but not even the kids believed that one.

I set up the tent in the front yard and outfitted it with air mattresses and proper bedding because if I wanted to sleep on the ground I would have stretched out across the driveway already. Chris, who thought we were saving the tent for the camping trips we never take, asked me to fold it up from time to time or at least move it around the yard so it didn't ruin the grass. He is quite protective of the grass, but I suspect moving the tent had less to do with our lawn and more to do with a growing concern that I may move into the tent permanently. I think the tip-off was the addition of proper lighting and wifi, and the banner ads for composting toilets that mysteriously started showing up on my laptop.

It is admittedly the best money I've spent in a long time. When you're in a tent, everything's all birds and breezes. You never want to go back inside to reality.

Reality looks nothing like the brochure from hospice, which the nurses assured me featured paid actors. You can tell they're actors because they are clearly not sleep-deprived. Non-actors would feature a middle-aged woman covering her children's ears while the elderly woman visibly swore a blue streak at anyone within reach. The photo on the back of the brochure would be of the family rifling through the hospice care package and taking the good drugs for themselves.

This, by the way, is why they send drugs in very, very small quantities. I used to think it was because the patient is on hospice and they don't want to waste any leftovers – which would be very New Englandy of them. Now I realize it's because the family will eventually be driven to take the drugs.

One nurse came on a particularly bad morning. She asked how things were going and I went into a rant which I won't repeat here.

"But how is she feeling?" The nurse said. "Is she comfortable?"

To which I say *how dare she*. How dare she express concern for her actual patient when I am so obviously on Google Maps looking for the best route to drive my car into a lake.

"Who the **** cares?" is what I wanted to say.

"Would you like to go see her now?" is what I did say.

Is it bad that I took comfort in my mother-in-law's equal opportunity hurling of verbal abuse? When the nurse came back out to the living room, she panic-dialed the pharmacy and said "we need better drugs." It's weirdly comforting to have a stranger empathize with you – especially after she has categorized you as a self-centered jerk.

But as comforting as the promise of new and stronger drugs is, it doesn't beat the tent. Having the tent is like being a kid and running away from home because no one understands you and they won't miss you anyway and won't they be sorry once you're gone. It doesn't take far – halfway down the driveway? The other end of the yard? – before you start to realize that you might have been wrong.

They might not understand you, but it's okay. They do miss you – and you miss them. And you will be sorry when they're gone.

So you go back with fresh eyes. Because sometimes you need to see things the way someone else sees them. And that someone is in a tent.

I get it from Nana, who erected a tent of her own in the midst of That Place. Every time we went to see her, she told us she had just finished doing one of her favorite things, from attending church meetings to giving a ballet recital. She introduced us to people whose names I recognized from her childhood. I had to give her credit for going to her happy place and staying there no matter what happened to her physical surroundings. To the untrained eye, she lost touch with reality, but in doing so made us question our own reality.

"Don't ever get old," my mother-in-law often told me. I don't think she had thought through the alternative. In her defense, she may have been referring to a state of mind, not an accumulation of years. What differentiates an annoyed old person from a pleasant old person? I discussed this with a friend who was also taking care of her mother, and came up with a few ideas.

Be flexible. Cranky people get stuck in their ways early on. If you want to be happy later, practice flexibility now. Try new food. Guard against dismissing ideas out of hand. Remember that change has always happened and it's not something new that's designed specifically to piss you off.

Be nice. This comes to some people more naturally than others, but it's never too early to start cultivating your inner nice person. I don't mean to lose your love of taunting your kids with embarrassing childhood stories in front of their friends. File that under *joie de vivre* and have at it. It's the taunting that goes on inside your head you have to be careful of. Watch the inner monologue because that stuff is going to come out loud and clear on down the line. Admit it: your filter's going to get clogged and you're just going to chuck it. Figure out what's behind the filter now so what comes out later is what you really want to be saying.

Start figuring out what's important. I am not high maintenance. I am not a neat freak. I have not once been mistaken for Miss Manners. But sometimes I flip out. And it's stupid stuff I flip out over. Nobody likes to be nitpicked, henpecked, or micromanaged. It's not a matter of stopping the flow of criticism, it's a matter of not letting stuff get you. My friend gives things the Five Year Test: if it won't matter in five years, let it be. "Don't sweat the small stuff" is cliche for a reason. There's stuff that's important now, but won't be later. If by the time my children reach a certain age they are still not putting their underwear in the hamper or are going out with their hair unbrushed, it's their spouse or friend or footman's problem. Not mine. My job of polishing the outside is done. It's time to enjoy what's inside.

Trust people who are trustworthy. Figure out who these people are before you start forgetting if you've had lunch or not. This is hard because the person you choose to help you make important decisions may have their own brain eaten by a zombie and start suggesting things that are not in your best interest. Do the best you can.

Remember all this. Write it down. Mark it on your calendar. Put sticky notes on your head. Do it until it's easy.

Old is as old does. When my mother-in-law tells me not to get old, I'm pretty sure what she means is not to get to the point where I can't get out of my own way, mentally. I figure I should start practicing now if any of this is supposed to do any good in the future. And if it doesn't? Then I will have been unnecessarily nice and friends will decide that zombies have eaten my brain.

At about the time I was at my least charitable, a letter from a mother to her daughter circulated the internet aimed at reminding adult children to have patience with their parents because they had been patient with them. I had no patience for it, and wrote my own letter.

Dear Firefly,

There are a few things you need to know, as well as a few things I need to remember.

First, you owe me nothing. You have always made my life a better place to be. Your work here is done.

If I am nasty, remind me what I always told you about how people will not be friends with you if you are mean to them. Somewhere along the line I may lose my common sense.

If I am slow, it may seem like I am paying you back for all the times I hit my head repeatedly on the steering wheel while it took you an agonizingly long time to get settled and buckled in the back seat. Please know that I'm not doing it on purpose.

Remind me that tantrums are not okay at any age.

If I expect you not to be frustrated with my memory lapses in the future, I need to start paying attention to you now. I need to listen so you know how important you are. If I listen to you now, you'll be able to tell the difference later between a memory lapse and just not paying attention.

I know I let you get away with some crazy outfits but please, reign me in early and often.

If you need to hang out with me for more than a few minutes, bring a book. I won't mind. I just want you with me. I used to do that when it took your brother 45 minutes to eat his lunch.

When it's time for me to stop driving, remind me to believe you.

I'm a little nervous about the technology thing, frankly. Remind me that change is good and that it will continue to happen no matter how perfect I think something was.

You were always fine with showers. It's your brother who screamed like it was holy water and he was the devil himself at bathtime. Make him deal with me if I develop a fear of bathing.

Feel free to add your own stuff to this list. I probably won't remember anyway.

But I won't forget how much I love you.

Love,

Mom

How not to feed people

There was this one time I almost poisoned my whole family.

At the end of our road there is a chestnut tree. One of my favorite things is foraging for food, so when I walked by and was hit in the head by a falling chestnut I recruited the kids and together we gathered an enormous bunch of chestnuts to roast. I washed them off because we do not just eat things off the ground, and then carefully scored them so they wouldn't explode in the oven. I think I have only ever exploded an eggplant in the oven and would like to keep it that way. While they were roasting I started to wonder why no one else had gathered the chestnuts and, growing suspicious, I googled "can chestnuts kill you?"

Which they can. The tree on our road is actually a buckeye, which will kill you. I should probably tell the neighbors because now I'm wondering if that's why the house down the street always has new renters.

I like being told what to do sometimes. Being told what to do means there's something else you don't have to do. This is why I love diets. To be clear, I don't love going on diets. I love the philosophy of them. I am partial to the ones that talk about food a lot. When one of my cooking magazines tells me to go on a diet and gives me a whole week of menus, I am in hog heaven. Who cares what they're telling you to eat when there are 21 meals you don't have to plan? One time there was a vegan diet in Vegetarian Times. I looked at the week's worth of food and decided that everything looked delicious and undisgusting so I went for it. On day two I realized it would take me a month and a half to get through the 21 meals.

Who actually eats the food they intend to eat? You buy the ingredients and then have toast for breakfast instead of the fresh fruit and soygurt with cashew crema because you woke up late and barely had time to pack the Buddha Bowl you had planned for lunch which will live in the break room fridge until the second coming of Christ because you forgot it was pizza day. As much as I like the idea of telling everyone I'm vegan for the week, I refuse to miss pizza day.

On Day Three I still had 20 uneaten, pre-planned meals to go. It's not cheating, it's economizing.

Before I finished those 20 meals, "The Hip Chick's Guide to Macrobiotics" arrived in the mail. I ordered it because a friend of mine invited me to take a macrobiotic cooking class with her, and then suggested I read this book ahead of time so I would stop asking stupid questions.

I still have no idea what macrobiotics are, but I did notice the quotes on the back of the book are from Gwyneth Paltrow's macrobiotic chef and Madonna's macrobiotic chef. So obviously what I need is not a book, it is a chef.

The best part of this cooking class was that it happened the day before my nephew came for a visit. On his last visit, this nephew was convinced we were feeding him cat food (it was lentils). He prepared for a week at our house like it was an episode of Fear Factor. The foray into macrobiotic cooking opened up a whole new arena of things to serve him – things like Millet Mashed "Potatoes" with Mushroom Gravy, despite my rule of thumb about avoiding food written with quotes around it. "Flan," for example. Faux foods aside, I'm pleased to have this book on my shelf. It looks impressive and implies that I'm a hip chick. It also implies that I'm a hypocrite and a poser, but whatever.

The class was fantastic and everything I had hoped for. Two lovely people made dinner for me and three other women, all the while explaining what they were doing and what each kind of seaweed was. And then we all sat down to dinner, at which point the hostess turned to me and said "so Susan, how long have you been vegan?" And I was so sad because I was starving and the food looked delicious and I thought for sure I was going to be asked to leave. So I kept my mouth too full to answer questions politely.

Really, I took the class in the same spirit I would take an Italian cooking class or a sushi class. I wanted to know what some of the ingredients were and how to use them. I needed some new recipes. And I wanted a night off. Okay, there. I've said it. I don't give two hoots about going macrobiotic. I just wanted a few hours of relative peace and a meal I didn't have to think up and make myself. Is that so much to ask?

The very next day my nephew arrived. On the way home from the airport he made me listen to the original Broadway cast sing "All Shook Up," prefacing this action by saying, "I know you hate musical theater, but...." I have never been more grateful for an entire pantry of things to feed him in retribution.

Firefly has always been an adventurous eater. She is the one who came up with capers in scrambled eggs, which is delicious, and peanut butter tomato sandwiches, which are not. She likes to experiment, applying the scientific method in the kitchen. Once I found a Sticky Note with "mango, cocoa powder, water" x-ed out, and the words "do not ever make this again" below. She's not only an adventurous eater, she is a good eater, keeping me on the straight and narrow when I would happily fall face first into a chicken pot pie.

She does not know about my salsa con queso problem. I've seen to that. A week or so ago I was at the grocery store and spotted some. I could not resist its charm, so into the cart it went. When I got home the house was full of people who have been led to believe I eat nothing but spelt and dark, leafy greens, so I did what any poser would do: I put the jar in my purse and smuggled it into the house. When no one was looking, I put it in a cupboard behind a jar of homemade applesauce.

A few days later, I was working late and suddenly remembered my stash. No one was awake. No one would know. I dove in. Ah, the spicy, gluey, goodness! This happened a few times over several days. Once I thought there was less in the jar than I had left, but what could I do? Ask around to find the culprit and risk giving myself away completely?

I usually put the jar in the produce drawer, where no one ever looks. The one time I didn't get it back into the produce drawer, Sketch found it.

"Mommy, what's this?" he asked, holding the jar aloft.

"I have no idea."

"Where did it come from?" he persisted.

"Did you get all your laundry put away?" Laundry has this amazing ability to halt everything and make people disappear, mid query.

And then we were at the grocery store, where I accidentally went down the chip aisle. "Mom," he said in a voice that carried to the parking lot, "You know that orange jar of cheese that showed up in our refrigerator? *This is where it came from.*"

Sometimes I take the family down with me. Once we went to the beach and got dinner from the clam shack. I never let the kids get stuff from these places when we're at the beach because I always pack a nutritious lunch in my picnic hamper and they will eat it, by golly. So this was the grand exception. We sauntered up to the window and ordered all manner of fried food.

And then we had a picnic. I went in for an onion ring and Sketch said "no! Don't eat that first! You have to eat your..." and we all looked for the thing that was supposed to pass as the nutritional linchpin. My kids surveyed the assortment of golden fried goodness in grave confusion. Was this dinner? Had they missed something?

We all have our moments. One day my sister called and asked what you do with flax seed meal. Before I could answer I had to regain consciousness, having passed out from the shock. My sister, the woman who bought packaged lunch meats *because* they have more preservatives, the woman who relentlessly mocked me for considering rice and beans a meal, the woman who has never heard of half the stuff in my pantry, bought flaxseed meal because it was on Oprah. I told her what she could do with it – and by that I mean sprinkling it on stuff and adding it to other stuff, not, you know, something else. And all I can say is, if Oprah can get my sister to eat flax seed meal, why are we not using her on some super secret diplomatic mission?

When my nephew was here we went to Trader Joe's so he could a) pick out things to eat when we were having Love Burgers with soy cheese and "bacon" on hemp buns and b) pick out a few things to send to his sister at camp.

I wanted to send a care package but didn't want to be that aunt who sends all the wrong things. I remember being 18 and thinking "*a check*! What is so freaking hard about sending *a check*?" So my nephew pointed things out that she likes and I tossed them into the cart. Turns out they were all things I like but try not to buy because I am not a teenager.

I got all the stuff home, put it in its own little bag and shook my boney finger at the rest of the family. "Do not eat! No! Bad! Down!"

And so it was safe until I found a box to put it in. I was not in a rush because she was going to be there all summer and I knew she had just gotten a care package from my sister. Always trying to outdo me, that one. Always wants her daughter to love her just a little more than she loves me.

A couple weeks later I found a shipping box but it remained empty because there was a *bear* at camp and we weren't allowed to send food to campers. For some reason they thought it was a bad idea for the kids to keep food in their cabins. Meanwhile my nephew joined his sister at camp and I, fraught with worry at the thought of those sweet children cohabitating with a bear, found solace in my niece's package of truffles. And then the chocolate covered pretzels.

I love bears.

How not to make a resolution

One year Firefly's homework was to neatly copy her New Year's resolution onto a piece of colored paper and hang it in the hall at school for district-wide parent teacher conferences. Her resolution was to clean up the house "because it's really messy."

You got the part about hanging it up in the hall at school, right? Fortunately Chris teaches a course in robots at her school, so I banked on the combination of mess and robotics to earn us a reputation among the academic community for being geniuses. Geniuses are often messy.

For the record, my resolution that year was not to clean up the house. My resolution was to make sure Firefly stuck to her resolution. For the last several years I've replaced resolutions with watch words. I've also replaced cleaning with living, but that's another story for another day. I can't tell you what my watch words are this year because that will jinx it and all hope will be lost. I can't tell you what they were last year, either, because I've usually forgotten what they are by April.

In my defense, I forget what they are by April because I've more or less incorporated whatever it is by then and/or given up completely. I do wish I could remember what they were because they were really good. Things like "courage," or "listening," or "remembering things," for example.

When I choose my watch words I cheat and pick ideas that are already in the works, so the ball is already rolling. The year I chose "say yes" (which I remember because of the truly terrifying things I said yes to), I had already agreed to a couple things way out of my comfort zone. Things like public speaking, public speaking, and public speaking.

My biological New Year starts sometime in September, so I get a sneak peek at what the theme of the year is going to be, and can acclimate to the idea before the rest of the western world makes their own resolutions. I think lots of people's biological New Year starts in the fall. It's the time of year we have all been conditioned to start new things.

I think that's why we make resolutions. It's because we do things in cycles. New Year is when we give a nod to things that come and go. We put on extra layers in the winter, we shed them in the spring. We learn and then we practice. We fear and then we embrace. We are messy and then we clean up. We teach our children the value of order and then we take a nap while they tidy up the place.

When I taught English to adult speakers of other languages I introduced my students to things like pranking people on April Fools Day, saying "rabbit, rabbit" on the first day of the month, and making New Year's resolutions. I was surprised how few of my students knew anything about these traditions. Talking about the kinds of things you might resolve to do and making a list of them made a great lesson. It was one of the most introspective and fruitful classes I ever taught. Students of course resolved to learn English, but they set their minds to do other wonderful things, large and small – though perhaps none as small as my own resolution to stop eating in my car.

I must have forgotten to convey the equal and opposite tradition of abandoning resolutions. Years later I ran into a couple from Guatemala who I had especially loved getting to know in class. They had made a wonderful life for themselves in a town not far away from me, and had recently bought a house. They reminded me that buying a house was the resolution they had made in class, and they didn't give up until they had done it.

Meanwhile, I still eat in my car. I think my resolution next year will be to listen to myself.

How not to be sick

The first time I ended up in the emergency room I was walking home from the Denver Public Library with Banana Yoshimoto's *Kitchen* in one hand and a street vendor bratwurst with sauerkraut and mustard in the other. I was crossing at the corner of 13th and Lincoln and the next thing I knew I was surrounded by people asking if I was okay. *Kitchen* was clutched in my left hand, while my bratwurst headed north on the windshield of a car.

I was hit by a cyclist who was trying to make the light. Lucky for him, he hit me instead of cross-traffic. I am more forgiving than a car – in so many ways.

Someone called 911 and the fire department arrived, despite my not being on fire. I said something like "hooray! Denver firemen!" and told them they were all just exactly as handsome as everyone said they were. One of the perks of having your bell rung is your filters of self-respect and self-preservation get knocked clean off. It's really easy to say what's on your mind. Which is why I had such nice conversations with the other patrons in the emergency room, who were mostly there with gang-related knife wounds.

When they admitted me they asked me important questions like who was President, what the date was, and why wasn't I wearing a helmet. I didn't know you had to wear a helmet to the library, but have made a point of it since and now see its charm.

The guy who hit me showed up at the hospital and waited with me until I was called. I noticed a music sticker on his helmet and realized he was the son of a concert promoter I grew up idolizing. He never came through on my requests to pay my medical bills, but he did call in the middle of the night a few times – once offering to get me into shows which to my mind was the perfect answer to everything. Elvis Costello tickets would make not washing my hair for six weeks totally worth it.

He never came through with concert tickets and I swore off getting injured from then on out. It just wasn't worth it, you know?

Things went well for awhile. A long while, even. I had two extraordinarily successful hospital stays, from which I brought home two extraordinarily adorable children. I made myself right at home at the hospital with Child A, availing myself of the kitchenette on the maternity wing and eating all the Lorna Doones I could manage. I had a suitcase full of mom pajamas and super cute things for both of us to wear home. I brought my own pillow, bathrobe, and lavender shower gel. For Child B I don't think I even unpacked, taking the Lorna Doones and the baby to go.

Whenever my mother-in-law apologized for asking me to take her to the hospital for something, I was able to tell her honestly that two of the happiest days of my life happened in hospitals. Which is why I went to my midwife when something appeared to be very wrong with me.

It all started when I adopted a dog. Our rescue puppy came home and four days later I lay down and didn't get back up. On Father's Day I went out to get a special something for breakfast and secretly hoped I would pass out in the produce section so I could be whisked away someplace where someone would take care of me. An emergency spa, for instance, since I was sure nothing was actually wrong.

For the sake of my husband, who was quietly freaking out, I felt I should do something and went to see a friend who is an acupuncturist. He checked my pulse, my meridians, my latitude, and my longitude and said he didn't see anything disruptive. Still, he said

I should get a medical diagnosis if I thought something wasn't right. Was there anyone in the medical field that I'd be comfortable talking to, he asked?

My midwife is the loveliest, most unflappable woman you'll ever meet. The friend who recommended her to me in the first place literally kept having kids so she could keep seeing her. I hadn't seen her in several years but she got me right in for an appointment, asking all the right questions about all the right kids. She then examined me and made some calls in her lovely, calm, all-is-well way. The next thing I knew I had an appointment with an oncologist, a surgeon, and a radiation doctor. It's a good thing I'm done having kids, because I am never, ever, ever going to a midwife again.

Meanwhile Tuba, still a puppy, didn't leave my side. She is really more of a "jump on the couch and eat the laundry" kind of a dog but during that time, The Days of My Immobility, she was devoted and downright sane.

She was the one I worried about first when I got the diagnosis. I had signed a contract saying that I would let the rescue center know if I was unable to keep the dog. I told Chris, "if anything happens to me and Tuba is too much for you, please call the rescue center first," because I had visions of my family getting taken to court for giving our dog away. That's how you think when things are going wrong. The shoe did not drop so much as fall down a really long flight of stairs. Just when I thought the shoe had reached a resting point, down it would go again.

My first two appointments were with the radiation and oncology doctors. In the process of completing all the paper work for the first appointment I went through several of those tiny boxes of tissues they have on hand for people who are just now realizing what's going on. Between boxes, they took my picture for their files. It's a beauty.

Those tissues, for the record, are made of wax paper. From radiation I went upstairs to oncology, where I took one look at the shelf of wigs and hats and had a full scale melt down. And then they took another picture of me.

That night I had a revelation. Even though most of what the doctors said sounded like incomprehensible buzzing, I felt like they could be trusted. I figured while they were taking care of my diagnosis, I could take care of the rest of me. Separation of church and state, if you will. They were killing off something that really had nothing to do with me. It was my job to protect the rest.

The next morning I listened to a lecture in the car on the way to meet my surgeon and arrived at her office a changed woman. Even the ID photo went well. In fact, if it weren't protected by HIPAA, I'd have it forwarded to the DMV. I was able to drive myself to my appointments, so I listened to all kinds of things and arrived at the center in high spirits. Over the course of a year I burned through piles of podcasts – 75 hours of them getting to radiation appointments alone. A friend gave me *Science and Health,* which I listened to in the car twice. The book ends with a chapter called Fruitage. Fruitage is made up of letters from people who read the book in the 1800s, describing what it meant to them and often what lengths they had to go just to get a copy. I listened to these stories from the comfort of my car on a device that held wisdom from the 5th century B.C. right along with David Bowie's last release.

The car ride was just the beginning of my newly discovered "me time." If you can see past the part where they fill you with toxins, cut you apart, and then cook you, long term medical treatment is practically luxurious. Once I arrived at the treatment center I'd curl up with a book in the reclining chair for a couple hours until my nurse told me it was time for Benadryl. There is no sense in trying to stay awake when someone is pumping Benadryl into you, so I opted for the afternoon nap. I also opted for the heated blanket, the green tea, and the homemade bread pudding. You know how I fantasized about passing out and being transported to a bucolic place where they'd be kind to me? The treatment center was it. They even asked about my shellfish allergy on several occasions, which either means that some of these appointments are catered or they got my hospitality rider.

In hindsight, I realize that had I fainted dead away in the produce section of my grocery store I would have been stuffed into an ambulance and taken to the emergency room – which is completely not like a spa. At all.

I was desperate not to miss a single treatment. For one thing, there was a finite number of them and I wanted to keep that number ticking down quickly. For another, it was a long drive and you don't find out that they can't give you your bread pudding and your afternoon nap until you arrive and they look at you. So once when I felt dehydrated between treatments, I went to the emergency room like they told me to. I quickly remembered that I had sworn off such things. Here's what happens in the emergency room:

1. The building sucks the life right out of your phone.
2. Time stops.

Before my phone died I called Chris and then lined up a friend to meet the kids after school should it take forever (which it did). I had to leave a voicemail for Chris, which gave me a moment of *déjà vu*. When I ended up in the hospital in Denver I had dinner plans with my boyfriend so I called him from a payphone and left a message saying "I'm in the ER, will probably be late for dinner." That landed so well I tried it again twenty years later on my husband.

Unable to get through to my cell phone, Chris freaked out and called the ER. They were apparently short staffed and those little cubicles with curtain dividers don't have private phone lines, which explains the angry ER nurse who told me to get my husband to stop calling. I didn't know what to do, so I did the only thing I could think of – I cried. And then I couldn't stop. That bag of saline they had dripping into me? It came right out my face. I realized (possibly months later) that my reaction had zero to do with the curt nurse. In fact, my trip to the ER may have had zero to do with being dehydrated. All I needed was a good cry.

I had several epiphanies while I was going through treatment, which I enjoyed sharing with my oncology nurse, Barbara. I figured she heard these bluebirds of inspiration often as her patients sorted through what they were feeling and experiencing. Your nurse is the person who knows more than anyone what you are going through. Since they are required by hospital protocol to listen, they are on the front line of hearing it all. I figure she could write a book with all the nuggets of wisdom she's gleaned.

In addition to telling my nurse, I took some notes so I could remember the high points of my journey later. I had known people who came through life-threatening experiences and were absolutely, unmistakably better for it. They were kinder, more understanding, and had a weird peacefulness to them. I worried that if that happened to me it might wear off before I could really cultivate my inner glow and be the envy of my neighbors. I wanted something to refer to if I needed a reboot. Here are my notes from the bolts of clarity I shared with Barbara:

"Having cancer is like having a dog."

"You can't lie on the grocery store floor with the voices in your head."

"The stupid cupcakes are actually not that important. Fondant is total overkill."

"Morning glories are pretty but I know they're just going to choke out my green beans."

"If you look at someone you might accidentally punch them."

"You don't realize you've been carrying a boat anchor until someone throws something at you."

I didn't feel I needed to elaborate *because obviously.*

Several months after treatment ended I was driving to work and suddenly had ideas about a story I was working on. Whole paragraphs popped into my head fully formed, like they used to. I had to pull over and write them down before they went away. That's when I realized it had been a little murky inside my head for awhile and maybe things weren't coming out as clearly as they could have. So to clarify:

Having cancer is like having a dog. One of the perks of cancer (a phrase you don't get to use every day) is that people go out of their way to stop and talk to you. There's something about the scarf/hat/sporty new buzz cut that breaks the barrier between us humans, and we say things to strangers that we'd normally never dream of saying. You know how easy it is to talk to a stranger about their dog? It's like that. If we see someone who has the same kind of dog we once had, or someone we love had that kind of dog, it makes us all fuzzy inside and we have to say something.

You can't lie on the grocery store floor with the voices in your head. When your thoughts have a tantrum, walk away. If your toddler throws himself on the floor at the grocery store, you don't get down there with him and scream in total agreement (although I'd pay money for that). Just like the toddler, the voices in our heads have bad days. Don't engage. They're just loud suggestions. Honestly, I think those tantrum voices are what got me into the chemo chair in the first place, but that's a whole different conversation.

The stupid cupcakes are actually not that important. This is an admittedly cheap shot at that Mom of the Year who is always showing up for everything with cupcakes. Science fair? World Explorers? Single cell organisms? She's got subject-specific, fondant topped cupcakes for all of them. Our lives are way too full, yet we beat ourselves up for not doing more. Being eight places at once is for the birds. Once you've had the daylights scared out of you, you stop caring what people think and start doing things because they're important or they make you happy, not because you think someone else thinks you should.

Morning glories are pretty but I know they're just going to choke out my green beans. Once we had a morning glory come up through the dining room floor. It was like an alien invader, sneaking through a series of tiny cracks overnight and heading for the nearest chair leg. Since then, morning glories have been my nemesis and I refuse to plant them. Sometimes I waffle because they're so pretty, but then I remember that they will inevitably strangle everything in sight. Sometimes we knowingly plant morning glories in our lives. We should probably rip them out, and then stop putting more in.

If you look at someone you might accidentally punch them. My daughter was in a play so lots of theater analogies came up that year. In fight choreography when you "punch" someone you look where you want your fist to go, not where you want it to look like it's going. Look past your colleague's head instead of at his or her nose or at some point your fist will follow your eyes and you will punch someone in the face. Yes, you may sometimes want to do this, but you should not. The point: focus on where you want to go, not where you don't, because that's where you're going to end up.

You don't realize you've been carrying a boat anchor until someone throws something at you. People say all the time that life threw them a curveball. I don't know much about baseball, but when anything gets thrown at me, I drop what I'm holding and cover my face. Sometimes you need that to happen in order to see what it is you've been carrying around. There were several times when I literally thought "I can't hold this right now," and set down a responsibility. I can never remember where I've left things, so to the best of my knowledge I have not picked those things back up.

Being sick is not awesome, but people are. It's amazing what they think to do when someone is in the midst of something mind-numbingly icky. We refer to these events as Casserole Situations, because that's the first thing people do for you. In addition to some killer lasagnas, people helped with rides, company, reading material, house cleaning, child care, a massage, and much, much more. People I barely knew cheered me on as my hair grew in.

My new hair felt like a bunny. People could not resist touching my head – kind of like how they won't keep their hands off a pregnant belly. In fact, my hair was soft like a baby's. One of the volunteers, who had talked me into getting a wig because they're easy and awesome and make you look like Laura Petrie, told me to keep it on hand for bad hair days. I have it next to the maternity pants I pull out on Thanksgiving, but I don't see myself using it. When your hair falls out in handfuls and then comes back in, there are no bad hair days.

I loved that volunteer. You really do form a bond with the people taking care of you. I think it's Stockholm Syndrome. My oncology nurse quit after I was done (I'm sure it's unrelated), and my surgeon moved to California. I think that's a good thing, because I had started to wonder if people ever became repeat clients because they loved the people who took care of them – like my friend and our midwife.

Having long term treatment is like being pregnant, except the life you get at the end is your own. Nausea, fatigue, months of waiting.

Sound familiar? Perhaps the reason treatment takes so long is it takes awhile to get all this into our cells, so not only are we not the same person at the end, but we've had a good long time to practice the new version of us. Things worth becoming are worth the time.

The treatment took nine months, and at the end of it I had a brand new life. Now that's a heck of a midwife.

How not to try on a bathing suit

For years I knew exactly what would fit and what would not. I bought swimsuits from catalogs, and off the rack without bothering to try them on. I figured if it was at least close to my size, it would work. That's why they're made out of stretchy fabric, right? It's swimwear, not rocket science.

The first problem I had was during my brief foray into surfing. I started by borrowing a friend's brother's wetsuit. He is bigger than me so the suit instantly filled with water, acting as both a drag chute and shelter for migrating sea life. It was also incredibly unflattering.

Before long I decided my new hobby warranted a wetsuit of my own, and I hit our local surf shop to pick one out. This was where I realized just how badly the first one fit. Wet suits are tight and hard to put on when you are standing in a tiny cubicle with no place to sit down. Which is how I lost my balance and, clutching at the dressing room curtain, landed squarely on the surf shop floor in my underwear with a wet suit around my calves.

This experience served me well years later when I was in a Victoria's Secret dressing room trying on a bra to make sure it worked under a bridesmaid's dress with a weird neckline. Firefly was two, so I took her into the dressing room with me. Unlike the surf shop, Victoria's Secret has nice doors on their dressing rooms – doors with just enough space for a two year old to crawl under and escape. Clutching random garments around me, I dashed out of the dressing room just in time to catch Firefly on her way past the cashier. I now shop small and locally because it's the right thing to do and because I cannot go back to that mall.

Shortly after that, I was in the market for a new swimsuit. I was having lunch with my friend Ken when I decided this and we set off to go shopping. Ken and I go way back. He has seen me through more break-ups than I will admit to having. He was my emergency back-up boyfriend when I had to go to events where I needed to not look like I was still single. If ever there was someone safe to go swimsuit shopping with, it was Ken.

We found a sporting goods store with stuff for both of us to look at, and I went to work. I took a few suits into the dressing room, and brought them back out. More in. More out. Finally, I found a really cute surf dress that I figured would work just fine for a day at the beach.

"Yeah," Ken said when I showed off my purchase. "I had a feeling that wouldn't go well."

Since then I've had dalliances with everything from tankinis to skirted mom-suits to full on kaftans. But my favorite suit du jour is my Speedo, which looks absolutely horrific on me. I got it because my then-current suit got tangled up around my ankles when I tried to swim laps.

Every ten years or so I get all hot and bothered about swimming. It is the one exercise that I not only do not loathe but actually enjoy. So when Sketch started swimming I decided I would use my time wisely and swim laps in a neighboring lane during his lessons.

Swimming is one of those things you can do until you're at least 109 years old, at which point you get to wear a swim cap that makes your head look like a hydrangea. I see people all the time at the pool who are well into retirement. Sometimes they can barely make it up the stairs into the gym, but once they're in the pool it's a whole different story. I want to be those people. The thing is, they're already swimming faster than me, so I think the time to start is now.

I went back to the surf store and tried on the largest competition-style suit they had because let's face it, I am not their target audience. As unflattering as it was, it covered everything important without making me look like a bound water balloon. It also promised to stay on as I heaved my way out of the pool, which made it a win in my book.

My first day back swimming I pulled a groin muscle. I had survived the pool and headed to the locker room, where I lost my balance trying not to touch any surface of the shower with any part of my body. Apparently I have balance issues. I also had issues figuring out that sweet spot between giving up too early and reserving enough strength to get out of the pool without mechanical assistance. These are the kinds of things you have to sort out before earning your hydrangea cap.

One thing I noticed is the big gap between swim team-aged swimmers and Team Hydrangea. At my gym, and probably others, there's a notable absence of 40 to 60 year old swimmers. If you've ever wondered why this is, put on a swim suit and walk past all your peers watching their kids' lessons. Swimsuits make leggings look like snow pants. It's mortifying until you realize no one is looking up from their phones.

At some point "I am not going out in public like this" gets replaced by "public schmublic." No one cares, and if they do they will be so wowed by your head to toe kaftan they will forget about the ill-fitting workout wear.

Take that, Ken.

How not to miss your own funeral

Shortly after I did not die, I had a big decennial birthday. I had planned to do something fun for this particular birthday, like get a group together and run off to an island, but I had already missed a lot of work so I had to make due with not dying.

My friends and family decided I needed a surprise birthday bash because as much as we all love each other, we may possibly love cake more. I was lured on a boat ride that ended at our local yacht club, where the mariachi band that met me on the dock followed me up the ramp and into the club, which I imagine is pretty difficult to do when you play an upright bass. They continued to follow me around as I greeted everyone I know, including out of state friends and family who were imported as a surprise.

I'm not sure which surreal aspect made me wonder if I had died and no one bothered to tell me. That seems like something I would do – die and not get the memo. Like continuing to show up at work after the company has gone out of business, wondering why no one has made coffee for months. I don't know how you find that kind of thing out, but if news of your own death comes as an email attachment, a 3rd class letter with no return address, or a call from an unrecognized number, I'm not going to get the message. Even so, it's likely to end up in a pile of permission slips and the sixteen pages of legal text in various languages that accompany letters from our health insurance company.

In our family, we don't so much have memorial services as throw parties. I say this as though we throw parties for dead people every third weekend of the month, but actually our experience is blessedly limited. My mom declared that nothing really changed at her passing and no commemoration of that nothing was needed. My mother-in-law made no such advance requests, but based on how she lived her life the family thought it best to throw a party – a "celebration of life" party, not a "spend it all on hookers and blow" party. At my mother-in-law's celebration we had flowers, streamers, balloons and party hats – all things she loved. Musicians who had fond memories of her putting up with them at the house turned out in droves, some playing songs they had written for her.

I, too, would like a party. I would like my friends to gather and say nice things about me. Maybe it could be a potluck and friends could make the recipes I shared with them over the years. Liz would bring my spinach jalapeño dip – hopefully remembering to secure the blender lid. My college roommate would bring the sun dried tomato and goat cheese penne I had long since forgotten. It would be a trip down memory lane for all of us. I mean them. There would of course be lots of pictures of me learning to walk, living as a ski bum, kissing a bronze boar in Munich, and sneezing birdseed at my wedding. Along with the photos would be people's favorite memories of me, 98% of which would be embarrassing because who has favorite memories that aren't?

All of these things happened at my surprise party, plus flowers, streamers, balloons and party hats, making me wonder if I was dead. I pieced it together, finding evidence to support my theory. For instance, my sister-in-law, who is good at everything and arranged the flowers at my mother-in-law's memorial service, made me an arrangement with the same number of white roses as my years. It was so giant it took up three-quarters of the table devoted to the guestbook and memorabilia. But perhaps the biggest "all signs point to dead" piece of evidence was that all this happened in the yacht club where my mother-in-law had her memorial bash. Furthermore, the only day that worked for that memorial service was Sketch's birthday, so musicians playing "Happy Birthday" at my party was startlingly familiar.

I cannot recommend this entire scenario highly enough. I think we should all high tail it to our friends' houses right now and regale them with the things we like best about them. It's such a shame to waste all that affection at an event where the person doesn't get to experience it and goes through the afterlife never knowing what they meant to people.

Or maybe they do.

How not to conduct an interview

Technology and I do not always get along. This was never more clear than when I started doing interviews for a music column and discovered that the sticky wicket was not artistic but technical. In what seemed like a matter of minutes we went from rotary dials to smart phones, with a dizzying array of apps and features in between. I have long been a proponent of gadgets knowing how to do everything imaginable. My expectations outran current technology for years before the lines crossed and technology sped out of sight. Once tech savvy, I am now officially old and in the dust.

The tech snafu that comes immediately to mind was a phone call with Dan Maines, the bass player for Clutch. I had prepared for it by researching voice recording methods for my super fancy flip phone and then testing them until I found one that worked. On the day of the call I was at a friend's house babysitting three kids – mine and a couple spares – aging from 18 months to three years. I got the kids busy with a project, made the call, and settled into what would be a pretty fun conversation.

Except the recording app didn't work. Fortunately I realized this right away and found a pen and paper. Imagine me perched at a kitchen island frantically taking notes, and then continuing to take notes following kids from room to room clutching sheaves of paper. Things then went smoothly for a few minutes – a sure sign that all three kids had filed into the bathroom where they were knee-deep in toothpaste and dental floss. I caught it before the kids completely encapsulated themselves, emerging later as butterflies. Too busy taking notes to stop them, I then watched as they emptied a large shipping box full of packing peanuts onto the kitchen floor and proceeded to swim in them. It's incredible what kids do when your mom voice is not available to you. When we got off the phone I did the most professional thing I could think of, which was to take a picture of the kids waist-deep in peanuts and send it to Dan's wife.

Chris is a sound engineer so he helped me sort out a recording device to use on later interviews. The model I use, a Zoom, has a pair of crossed microphones at the top that make it look like a taser. I find this puts interview subjects right at ease. It's a device that professionals use and it has many more menu options than I care to learn about. It is so professional, in fact, that I loan it to Chris from time to time.

I used the Zoom when I interviewed Cat, a radio host whose local music show, The Cheap Seats, was first to play a track from Meghan Trainor when she was in high school. I went to the station and spent about 40 minutes with Cat, talking about local music and how one lead singer fell off his bed during her phone interview with him live on the air. I couldn't wait to get home and transcribe the interview – except it wasn't there. I could see the file, but I couldn't hear anything. Chris explained that the setting I used told the Zoom I had plugged in a microphone so it didn't bother using the internal one. At least I think that's what he said. Chris doesn't know how to speak slowly and use small words so I do the best I can with his explanations. From what I understand I recorded 40 minutes of silence, creating an astonishingly large file. I called Cat, explained my idiocy, rescheduled the interview, and sold 40 minutes of silence on Etsy.

Silence is not generally my problem. One interviewee remarked on the sound of birds in the background as we talked. I told her I had my window open, rather than explaining the eight baby chickens in my bathtub. Another phone interview was done in a carful of people, pulled over in the shade near a Target. Sometimes the interruptions happen when I'm transcribing. I stop the recording, take off my headphones, say "what?" loudly, get no answer and go back to transcribing. I rewind a couple seconds and repeat the process with increasing volume until I realize the voice is on the recording, not in my house.

The first time I interviewed Dan Lombardo was for The Magazine of Yoga. Dan was a theater colleague and I thought it was interesting, if not outright oxymoronic, that he was a Buddhist and a director. As soon as I had set up the recorder, he implied he was going to mime the interview. If you listen to the recording the first thing you hear is me saying "Dan Lombardo, you are a jerk." The second time I interviewed him we were in my dining room. The interview process went much more smoothly until the cat jumped on the dining table. I yelled "get off, you disgusting animal!" to which Dan instantly shouted into the recorder "I didn't touch her!" I have not ruled out a third interview but Dan probably has. Even Buddhists have their limits.

How not to have personal space

No one went into my mother-in-law's bathroom if they could possibly help it. It wasn't that we honored the sanctity of her personal space. It was that we never knew what we were going to find there. Or we did know, and didn't like it. Dentures in the sink were the least of it.

When she passed on it was literally over a year before we used her bathroom. The four of us had shared one bathroom all our familial lives, so it wasn't like we were actively avoiding anything. You don't take advantage of something you've forever denied the existence of.

Then one day I decided I needed my own bathroom away from people who don't put the cap on their toothpaste and lo and behold there it was. It's not the weirdest bathroom in the house, but it is the ugliest. It has vintage vinyl paneling, original linoleum, and non-skid tub strips carbon dated to the '70s. We went in with a contractor bag and took everything out that wasn't attached to plumbing including the lights because they offended my bathroom esthetic. Taking out light sources is what we do. Chris got in there and bleached the daylights out of every surface. It didn't look different when he was done, but at least we knew it was "clean," and with the lights gone we couldn't see it anyway.

I moved in. I brought in a waste basket no one wanted and put up the shower curtain discarded by my family when they found one they liked better with the Periodic Table on it. The hooks on the back of my new bathroom door held two robes, my swimsuit, and a 1960s terrycloth beach cover up of my mom's I can't bear to part with but won't be caught dead in.

I like having my own bathroom and should have kept the gloating to myself. Before long people started migrating into my shower, discovering the once loathed hand-held shower head was not so bad after all. Not only that, but in my bathroom the shower curtain was not icky and there was no toothpaste in the sink. I tried to explain that my bathroom is less gross because they do not use it, but they refused to see reason.

Why the sudden interest, I wondered, when none of us would go within five feet of it before? How could I bring back its repellant qualities, without repelling myself? What was my version of dentures in the sink? The answer was obvious: feminine hygiene products.

I don't fear getting old, but I do fear all the stuff that comes with it. In its previous incarnation my bathroom was a fully plumbed, well decorated worst case scenario. "Look!" It said, indicating the dentures. "You'll lose your teeth!" It said other things too, but I'll leave those to your imagination. In short, the bathroom epitomized everything I didn't want to be.

Which makes me wonder, why are men so horrified of feminine products? Are they afraid they'll need them someday? That they'll get on my cycle, or suddenly notice their ear hairs need tweezing? What omens could possibly be haunting them? *They're men.*

I went to the grocery store and stocked up on everything I could find, including some things I had never heard of. I got maximum strength anti-itch cream, triple action anti-fungal ovule inserts, and feminine wash, in addition to economy size boxes of my usual sanitary supplies. Bonus points were given to things that came with applicators. As a nod to my bathroom's glory days I took a spin through the adult incontinence section, which is located across from feminine hygiene as if this sort of hijinxery happens all the time. Never have I been so grateful for self-checkout, although I could have done without the computerized voice saying "move your...Vagisil

Daily Intimate Wash Odor Block...to the belt." I then left adult diapers and everything else unwrapped on my sink, the back of the toilet tank, and the edge of the tub.

It took them a surprisingly long time to notice, but eventually they did and Chris set to work fixing the hall bath. The main reason no one wanted to shower in there was the hole in the ceiling, which served as a sort of Oregon Trail for generations of spiders. I don't think the hole was cut on behalf of the spiders, but it happened so long ago I don't honestly remember. Because things take time, I left my new sanitary products on display in my own bathroom as an insurance policy while work in the hall bathroom was in progress.

When Chris fixes Sheetrock he does it to exacting specifications. There's a whole system of waiting for things to dry, sanding them, and repeating the process. For days we had a bucket of Chris's supplies in the bathtub, plus the Shop Vac in the middle of the floor. It's just us, though, so it didn't matter that half the Shop Vac was sticking out into the hall. No one bothered about the Shop Vac doubling as the bathroom door until an exquisitely polite 10 year old visitor was found standing in the hall, legs crossed, wondering what to do. Does he move the vacuum? Does he use the bathroom and hope no one walks down the hall while he's in there? Does he wait until he gets home?

And then, from across the house I heard the five worst words in the English language. "You can use my mom's," Sketch told his unsuspecting friend.

This is why we can't have nice bathrooms.

How not to raise children

Before sitting down to write this section I tip-toed down the hall to peek in on the kids while they slept. They were so cute – all relaxed and floppy, with little smiles on their sweet faces. It made me want to shriek "get up! get up NOW!" at the top of my lungs because the child-shaped dents in the ceiling would have made me giggle for years.

I didn't because I am good at keeping up appearances and the appearance du jour is Responsible Mother.

Don't take this the wrong way, but even when Chris gave me a new vacuum for Christmas, marriage never made me want to walk into the middle of the cranberry bog and hold my head under water the way I wanted to when I first became a mom.

When you marry someone, you've probably spent some time with them (unless you've been sold into marriage, in which case you can skip this part). You know their quirks. You know, more or less, what you're in for. Marriage is a refuge. It's where you go at the end of the day, where someone is on your team and they always pick you first for theirs. You know that, as much as you never would, you can always leave. It's like holding someone's hand.

Becoming a mother is not so much holding someone's hand as having a nine inch spike driven through your foot into a ship's anchor. Suddenly, you can't go anywhere. Literally. You're supposed to keep this baby home for the first two weeks and unless you have someone to help you, you can't even go buy your own feminine products because that leaving the baby in the car thing? Frowned upon. And you do need help. Because as much as you love love love this person you are holding, it is like nothing else you've ever experienced. Everything up until this point has been quitable. Put downable. A baby? Not so. No matter what you do, no matter where you go, you are this person's parent. There is no way to walk away from that anchor unless you do yourself physical harm. Which you may or may not consider.

And then one day, you discover that the spike doesn't hurt. You are, in fact, quite mobile. You discover that what you thought was a rusty chunk of iron holding you is more like a scooter. You go places you didn't think of going before. Simple, daily things become bright and shining. You meet other people who are also on scooters. You move through life with more direction and purpose than you may have before. You and the scooter move as one - most of the time.

Yes, there are still things that are hard to do in your new circumstances. Nightclubs are awkward on a scooter. Railroad tracks are impossible. You work around these things, because the person who's come to live at your house fills you with such delight that he/she eclipses everything that came before. Including your privacy, your peace, and your sanity. You realize you haven't thought about sawing off your own limbs in weeks. You do not, after all, drown yourself across the street. You think maybe a second 9" spike through your foot would be a good idea. Just to be safe.

Once you get over lack-of-separation anxiety, other anxieties move in because psyches abhor a vacuum. This is in addition to the "how will I protect my child in the End of Days" anxieties that come from nowhere.

When Firefly was turning four I spent all day making her birthday party invitations. They had to be just right, with lots of pink and some kind of fairy motif. But mostly, they had to be unusual and artistic and cleverly thought out because who cares if Firefly and her friends like them? It's the other moms I'll be judged by.

Several of the invitations went to kids whose families I didn't know. This was an unnerving development. At four, Firefly had friends who were not the offspring of my friends. Those new friends had parents who would be opening those invitations, coming to our house, and eating the cake. I may as well put a photo of myself on Hot or Not in a string bikini.

Will they like the cake? Is their house cleaner/bigger/nicer/less broken than ours? What will they think when they drive up and meet us in all our glory?

Plan A: They will think what I convince them to think. They get the invitation, look it over and say "oh, they are those *artistic* people. I bet their house is a holy mess because that's how creative people live. Look how creative they are! Ooh, I hope they let us inside to use the bathroom! I wonder, do they have a bathroom?"

Plan B: There is no Plan B.

Looking back at those invitations, they weren't even that creative. Before we had Martha Stewart, Pinterest, and other rings of hell they were Darned Creative. But now, not so much. I didn't do any stenciling or cut silhouettes or have an origami hummingbird fly from the envelope when opened. Their one redeeming creative characteristic is that they didn't come from the grocery store.

In addition to trying to form parental opinions, I made the invitations so I could have something to put in Firefly's keepsake box. The keepsake box is sort of like the running log you keep when you are thinking about firing someone. It's evidence. So when she gets older and starts complaining about her childhood I can trot out all the things in her keepsake box. Look at what I did for you! How can you possibly *still* be complaining about sleeping in a drawer when I made these awesome invitations?

It is good to be prepared.

I am also beefing up the photo albums for the same reason. The kids love flipping through them, and if they look through them enough they will come away with the impression that their lives were never dull and they never had to go to bed or take baths. Look, you used to take baths in a wading pool on the lawn with six of your closest friends!

Or maybe I'll get sued – both by my children and the people who actually created the fairy motif I pilfered.

Some of the photos in their album are at the skating rink. Oh, the fun we've had skating! Just look at us! We live at the beach, but sometimes we go skating in June just to be contrarians. Or as Firefly explained to Sketch on the way, "we're going ice skating because our house is too messy to have a play date at home." I'm hoping she said it because I'm always "augh! playdate! to your stations!" and not because she looked around and said to herself "there is no way I'm inviting a friend over."

We showed up at the rink to meet Firefly's friend Emma and her mom and rent skates. I have owned several pairs of skates in my life, but managed to keep none of them in case I had kids. This is because skates now look exactly like skates then and it's important only to make your children wear things that are spectacularly dated yet completely worthless on eBay.

Firefly and I headed gamely for the ice while Emma's mom followed along with Sketch. Despite having grown up skating, I am only now aware that I am on ice surrounded by children with sharpened knives on their feet. "Brave for the kids, brave for the kids" I chanted inside my head as I clutched Firefly's hand. She was between me and the wall, with a ridiculously huge smile on her face, blissfully unaware of the crushing force on her little hand.

Gwen, who is of course a graceful skater because she is good at everything, followed with Sketch. Sketch had a fine time, tippity tapping his feet along the ice as she held him up like an under-stuffed teddy bear. He wouldn't stand up on his own because then she might have let go. Sketch may be many things, but stupid is not one of them.

After peeling my fingers from her hand, Firefly made her way around the rink with little Emma. Emma was wearing a darling skating dress and carrying an American Girl doll which was also wearing a darling skating dress. Firefly sported jeans, gloves, and a pillow-top mattress pad with memory foam. Now I want to make an American Girl-sized pillow-top mattress skating outfit.

When Sketch had enough I felt it was important to validate his feelings of enoughness and ran to the car before Firefly could sign up for skating lessons. On the way home the heavens opened, at which point I remembered that one of Sketch's friends was camping nearby for the week. I called the mom's cell phone and left a message about our dryer being vacant and our living room being available. And then we piled inside, where I looked around and yelled "augh! playdate! to your stations!"

One winter day Firefly came in from playing in the snow and asked if they could sled. I said yes, because I'm nice. And then I said no, because the hill shoots right down onto the road. And then I said no again because we have no sleds.

"Yes, we do," she said.

"No, we don't"

"Yes, we do."

"Fine," I said. " Sled then."

I watched as she grabbed a snow shovel, sat in it, held onto the handle, and went sledding down the hill, being careful not to shoot out into the street. Her friends grabbed the other quadrillion shovels we have lying around the yard and zipped down the hill after her. And then they found the top to the sandbox and used it as a saucer. And then our upstairs neighbor Randy came home, saw what they were doing, and proceeded to sled down our hill on his cooler. That's not a euphemism. The kids thought he was the awesomest and on this we are in solid agreement.

Add to the undeniable wonder of Trout Towers:

1 sledding hill

7 white trash sleds

1 X-treme Cooler Glider

There are things I learned in elementary school that I will never forget. Extra-curricular things like "stop, drop, and roll" or how to rescue someone who's fallen through the ice. I stop, drop, and roll whenever so much as a spark flies out of the fireplace. Also when I set the toaster on fire. The broken ice thing I've had less experience with. Which is good.

One day Randy came by and asked to borrow an aforementioned shovel so he could clear a little spot on the pond across the street. He had his skates with him and a bucket to sit on while he put on his skates. He was obviously a Boy Scout in a former life and had thought of everything. He asked if the kids would like to come with him, for a little boot skating.

We bundled up, comically. Sketch could barely lower his arms. This was to guard the kids against the cold, as well as the ravages of the brambles that circle the pond. "Be careful," said Sketch. "Some of the flowers are pointy."

As we approached the pond, the ground started to give way under us and we broke through little pieces of swamp ice into a couple of inches of pooled water. This made me nervous. After all, if these shallow pools were not thoroughly frozen, why should the pond be trusted?

We caught up to Randy, who had by then shoveled the near end of the pond. He came to the edge, and the ice crumbled underneath him - again into about an inch of water. I turned to Firefly. "If you hear any cracking sounds, lie down on the ice and pretend you are floating like a star." She decided not to go.

Sketch, after evaluating the solar gain of shallow water pooled on dark earth and then doing a quick bit of calculus to determine pond depth and water temperature, scurried after Randy. He had a ball while Firefly and I watched, carefully listening for the zipping sound of ice giving way. I mentally scoured our house for the closest ladder, which is ridiculous because it would take me 10 minutes to get to the house, find the ladder, and return. I should have brought one with me. And some rope. And maybe some water wings. Then I recalled the suggestion to make a human chain and crawl out onto the broken ice. Which is great except this human chain would be made up of me and a six year old.

"I want him to come back in now," said Firefly.

"It's okay," I assured her. "If the ice broke, Sketch would be up to his waist in cold water."

It is completely irrelevant that Randy, a very grown-up man, is zooming around out there and Not Falling Through. It is irrelevant that the ice is obviously Very Solid. It is irrelevant because now it is my child we are talking about and there was that one time in the third grade when we watched the safety film on frozen ponds and Sketch, why are you not cold yet?

Seeing that nothing was happening to either of the men-folk, Firefly went out onto the pond – at which point I graduated from ladders to human chains to simply throwing myself into the hole created by my children.

Finally, Sketch was cold. I tried to say something like "oh darn, already?" but instead tucked a child under each arm and headed for dry land. Now that it's over, I wish I had taken a moment to breathe in the winter air and watch little people sliding around a tiny pond and making ice angels. But I'm still really glad it's over.

Chris does not understand my parental angst. In his defense, it is a many-layered angst, on which graduate-level psychology courses are based. Still, you'd think he'd learn. When I took Firefly to a birthday party which featured several other five year old girls ranging from pleasant to completely psycho, Chris asked, "so how was the party?" in a "hey, how were those front row Red Sox seats?!" tone instead of a "how did washing the cat go?" tone.

That was his first mistake. His second mistake was waking me up to ask me. So I told him. I told him about the girl who screamed "*I don't like yellow birthday cake! I will only eat white!*" when she was offered a slice. I told him about the petite peanut who repeatedly body slammed another girl in the bouncy house, literally dragging her out by her hair.

I went on and on until Chris had fallen asleep. And then I told him some more. I told him tales of derisiveness and deceit. I told him of pony ride heartbreak and the unnerving gusto with which children swing a bat at Dora. Boy howdy do they need the candy inside that piñata. In short, it was not exactly the way I would have chosen to spend my afternoon.

Sometimes people who appear to be having the most fun are holding onto a scrap of sanity and keeping their eye on the prize (bedtime). At pool parties I spend the entire time making sure they're not drowning. When I get home I wonder why I'm starving and realize I forgot to eat. Or breathe.

What I think is interesting is how easy it is to figure someone else has it easier. I do this to my mom all the time. She'll mention that I should do something that she herself doesn't have time for and I respond with "What? *You are retired*."

The other day when I was feeling reasonably on top of the world a total stranger looked at me and said "wow, you look beat." And I whacked him with my handbag. Seriously, who says something like that? Sometimes I feel like we're expected to look tired or we're not doing it right. I get this aura of "don't worry about me, I'll be fine. I'll just carry these 75 pounds of groceries myself" when really I'm just bringing in the milk. There's this cultural thing that makes us feel like we're not contributing enough if we're not completely wrecked at the end of the day.

Mornings are atrocious, mostly because the robot vacuum does not make lunches. I pull out of the driveway late and in a state of nervous collapse, carrying two lunch boxes, two school bags, a change of clothes, after school sport bags, a computer, and my lunch. I shove it all in the car and close the door quickly so nothing spills out.

I close the door so quickly that sometimes I forget something. One morning I was driving along and out of the corner of my eye I noticed Sketch standing up in the back seat. Failing to buckle child into carseat = potentially indictable maternal failing. To which I say, at least I didn't leave him on the roof of the car.

When Sketch was an infant I had a fear of leaving him in his baby bucket on the side of the driveway when I left in the morning to take Firefly to school. His car seat was right behind the driver seat where I couldn't see him, so rather than ask Firefly if we had indeed remembered to put the baby in the car I'd ask her "how's your brother doing?" She'd look over at him and say "sleeping," and I'd know I had made it another day.

I keep these things to myself because I don't want to give them nightmares. I don't want to give them nightmares because I am the one they come to at 3 a.m. When Firefly was little, she had night terrors. To the uninitiated, "night terrors" means that you wake up screaming, but aren't really awake and whatever is making you scream is still very real. You are too caught up in the nightmare to wake up. In other words, night terrors are a metaphor for life.

Being new at this, we didn't know how to deal. Your kid screams and you go in and hold her, right? Except she's not awake and in her reality, the giant squid she's been screaming about has just rushed into her bedroom and grabbed her. It's maybe even making her scream extra loud because a giant squid that calls you "sweetie pie" and runs its slimy tentacles through your hair is just plain creepy.

Thanks to the pediatric advice of Google, we learned a little bit about what we were dealing with and could approach it with more finesse. Which means, we didn't touch her. I'd go in and use my best exorcist voice to let her know I was scaring off the scariness. Or I would say "Firefly! you're not afraid of it!" until she believed me. Or I'd tell her she was smarter and stronger and better than "it." And then I'd sing to her and run my slimy tentacles through her hair and tell her it was all gone. We stopped trying to wake her out of the dream, and started changing her experience within the dream.

I wish it were always this easy. I wish, for instance, that when someone is freaking out at work we could jump into whatever is going on in their head and set things right. Instead, we jump into whatever they've got going on and get stuck there.

Firefly eventually outgrew it, and we were pleased to note that Sketch was not following in her footsteps. Until he did. One night we heard the familiar screams and went to go administer the pep talk.

But where Firefly screamed her little lungs out, Sketch was saying something almost intelligible.

Sketch (sobbing, gasping, screaming): "Don't take my lunch!"

When Sketch was seven and offered to make dinner I considered sitting in the kitchen snacking the whole time he cooked, saying I wasn't hungry when dinner was served. For the record, I had the full support of the internet when I announced this as my plan. Random strangers made suggestions for style points, including announcing starvation 15 minutes after dinner and eating an entire box of cereal with all the milk in the house poured on top. That's the nice thing about the internet. You realize that even if you're still the most horrible person in the room, you're in really good company.

When Firefly (who is the nicest person in the family) hauls off and punches her little brother, I want to applaud her for waiting so long. It's not that I condone violence, it's that I can't fathom where she gets that kind of patience. No official statistics are available, but I'm guessing for each time she does go for the smack down, there are 37 billion times she resisted the urge. He's a little brother, after all. (A little brother who has offered to make dinner. Let us not forget where our bread is buttered.)

It's possible that Firefly is looking ahead, realizing her scrawny little brother will eventually be bigger than her. She is currently saving for a house, so this kind of planning is not out of character. I'm sure she learned all this from me because I am a shining example of how to do everything right. I taught them that it's bad to leave paychecks in the pocket of your jeans when you wash them, and that cell phones aren't for sitting on, and bees have personal space issues.

It was Chris who taught them not to make a u-turn across a median in front of a police car, but I covered the rest. Teaching by example is my forté. What is it I want them to learn from me? I want them to learn to cook so I don't have to. I want them to use their words. I want them to do unto others as they would have others do to them, assuming they don't turn out to be masochists. I also want them to know that I'm usually right and sometimes they are jerks, but I haven't figured out a bumper sticker slogan for this yet. What I suppose I really want is for them not to be jerks, listen when I ask them to do something, and stop eating loaves of toast before dinner.

Like Firefly strategizing for the future, we have to pick our battles. Yes, refusing to eat the dinner he worked so hard on would have given my son a window into my blackened and bitter soul. It may have helped him understand why my head spins around and orange sparks shoot out of my eyes when he eats a loaf of toast in lieu of dinner. Or, he might wonder why he is cooking for this mess of ingrates and throw in the towel, never cooking again because what a waste of time is that? You put all the effort into finding recipes that the whole family will like, making sure it is balanced and nutritious as well as sustainably grown, locally sourced, organic, in season, and aesthetically pleasing and then you offer up this meal that may as well be your heart and soul on a platter and they can't even take their own dishes to the kitchen when they're done.

Ahem. Anyway....

When my son made dinner, I set my eye on the prize and did not sit on the kitchen floor eating cheesypuffydoodles as planned. If I can help make cooking dinner a success for him, I figured, he may cook again. When two of my favorite things faced off, being fed trumped being smug.

In lieu of snacks, I used the opportunity to model the behavior I wanted to see. When it sounded like dinnertime was close, I asked Sketch if I could help by setting the table and then placed forks, spoons, and chopsticks at each place because I have no idea how we're supposed to eat noodles and jam.

Now here's a conundrum. We model the behavior we want to see, and then we lie to them about how delicious dinner is. It's not the first time we've lied to them, and it certainly won't be the last. Case in point: Santa and the Tooth Fairy.

What are you supposed to do with kids' teeth once they come out? I know the part about trading it for a buck, but then what? You can't send them to people because mailing body parts is a federal offense. So what do you do? Make jewelry?

The last time Firefly lost a tooth I only had a five in my wallet and I can't give her that or she'll expect an increase retroactively. A child has 20 baby teeth. I can't do math but that just doesn't seem like a good scenario financially. Unless you're her, and then it totally works.

So I took a dollar out of her piggy bank. Don't worry, I put a bunch of quarters in the pig to make it up to her. I don't know why, but the tooth fairy shouldn't travel with quarters. They would weigh her down and it makes the whole thing less believable. Ethereal being who comes at night and gives a dollar for discarded body parts? Totally believable. Rig her up with a roll of quarters and you lose all credibility. Although there was that one time I stuck a can of tuna under the pillow and no one batted an eye. Firefly is hip to the tooth fairy but too smart to out her because she's still cleaning up on lost teeth. Sketch, however, is all in.

I'm generally pretty straightforward about things with the kids. We try to walk the line between telling the truth and not being the ones on the playground that send other kids home in a state of existential angst.

One year when we passed a Toys for Tots bin, Firefly stopped, thought about it, and said "maybe Santa is all of us." Brilliant, right? I don't know where she gets it. Since then we've been off the hook with Firefly, who still gets presents from Santa because how else do they get their new December toothbrushes and rolls of tape? We are not off the hook with Sketch.

Sketch wants desperately to believe. He loves the idea of the Elf on a Shelf, no matter how many times we point out that surveillance is creepy no matter who is doing it. When we finally made the elf disappear, we told Sketch he gave up and went home. This will probably come back to bite us, like the time Sketch told a visitor that the Joseph in our crèche had gone for cigarettes. At the time it seemed kinder than telling him Joseph had been eaten by the dog.

It will be so much easier when I finally come out and tell the truth, or when they piece it all together, like Firefly's crowd-sourced Santa. And then I start wondering if there are some truths I haven't been told yet. Maybe some day I will pass a Toys for Tots box that makes all my self-invented explanations fall away and I will see things clearly as they are. I hope it doesn't ruin everything.

Knowing what to do at each stage of life is hard. It reminds me of the ceramics class I took my senior year of college because it was supposedly easy and fun. It turns out I don't have a gift for ceramics. Have you ever thrown a pot? On a wheel, I mean, not at someone.

When you're first learning, you find that if you have centered it properly and don't use too much force, you can make the clay take the shape you had in mind. It's kind of magical to watch. A lump turns into a lump with a dent. The dent gets deeper and becomes a cup. You keep it centered and push just enough, and something wondrous happens. Then you look up for a second and the next thing you know, it's gone all wobbly and clay is flying and you have no idea what you're holding in your hands.

That's the point we're at raising the kids. I make sure we stay centered. I keep my hand in it, but not too firmly. I encourage them to grow by pushing just a little.

I thought I would always know how my kids were shaped. I thought they would always be who I thought they were. Then one day you realize that your kid is more of a bowl than a cup. Look up again and you see they've given themselves a spout and a handle. I'm not ready for them to show signs of being someone I didn't anticipate, something that's beyond my control.

For years, since I was a child, I imagined what my children would be like. I pictured them acting the way I pictured them. And to some extent, they do. Or, more likely, I've adjusted my picture without realizing it. But from time to time, I notice that what I am looking at does not jive with the picture in my head. My kids are like no one I've ever known or imagined. I think Sketch is a cup but he's really more of a mug. Firefly is obviously a vase, except she has sprouted a handle and is insisting on being useful.

Maybe it's me that's going all wobbly, flying across the room. As for Firefly and Sketch, they are – and always have been – exactly who they're supposed to be.

How not to live in a plastic suitcase

One year at Christmas my parents proved once and for all that they love my sister more than me: They gave her Kiddletown. I can't think of anything I envied more. It was a suitcase which, when opened, contained a row of plastic-molded houses and stores with perfectly appointed plastic-molded gardens and pathways in front. I think there was even a playground or lily pond. It was lovely.

Kiddles were these delicate creatures – about two inches tall with tiny, tiny bodies and large heads and long, flowing hair. A lot of them were themed, as described in the tiny booklets that came with them. My sister had one that lived in a plastic case shaped like a perfume bottle, draped in lily of the valley. She was beautiful. I had a King and Queen of Hearts, a grandfather, and a middle aged housewife with bobbed blonde hair. Mom let us have Kiddles in lieu of Barbies. Not only were all a Kiddle's visible attributes right there in their oversized heads, but there weren't a ton of clothes, cars, or other accessories to purchase for them. If you wanted a different outfit, you bought a different Kiddle. What you see is what you get with a Kiddle.

Since there wasn't one available commercially, I made my Kiddles a camper out of a Saltine cracker box. I put plastic wrap where the windshield would be, cut in a door, and called it good. Once the Kiddles were stuffed inside the empty box, I imaged them in a spectacularly appointed home away from home. There were turquoise flowered vinyl booth seats with a kitchen table shaped like a daisy and a lava lamp hanging over it. There were bunk beds in back, shag carpeting, and a pool table. They must have had a full kitchen in there because once they all got onboard, that camper didn't stop for anything.

By the time I moved onto trolls, my engineering skills had improved. I built my troll family a luxury spread constructed from shoe boxes stapled together and glued to a piece of plywood, complete with gardens and a deck. It was lovingly decorated with handmade furniture and featured a kitchen, dining room, library, den, and anything else I felt like stapling on. The details were amazing, including my inspired use of dry chickpeas as biscuits in their pantry. One cannot in good conscience call it lovely, but it was very fun to build and play in. I think the trolls were happy there.

It's the chickpeas that made me realize what happened: I am here eating chickpea biscuits, while my sister lives in Kiddletown. I'm surprised I didn't see it before.

My first solo apartment was a studio condo at the foot of a mountain in a ski town. It looked like one room, but there was more than met the eye – as friends witnessed when I took them on a tour. I'd walk them through the apartment one way, and then take them back to the door, reassigning rooms as I went. The kitchen became the formal dining room. The closet where the cot was folded became the guest room. The bathroom became the guest bath.

It was a beautiful condo – in real life, I mean, not just my made up version. There were french doors to a balcony, and a stone fireplace in the corner of the living room. At night, I would lie on my fold out couch and pretend it was not my living room, but an actual bedroom complete with balcony and fireplace. I would watch the snow fall and think about how lucky I was. Like the Saltine camper, my condo could be anything I wanted once I was stuffed inside.

I have moved six times since then, not including long-term freeloading at friends' houses between cross-country moves. I have learned not to swear that I will never move across the country without a job and a place to live again in the same way that I've learned not to swear off waitressing. In my experience as soon as you swear something off the universe hands you an apron and keys to a rental truck. When I moved from Denver one friend told me I had to stop moving or stop buying books. That was my second to last move.

When I first landed at Trout Towers it was like the beginning of my troll house: Lovingly handmade, yet randomly stapled together. Over time we added what we needed, fixing things up as we went. A guest once asked me what I would do if I could get all our repairs and renovations done at once. At first the answer was obvious: faint, and then get out the list as soon as I regained consciousness. But then I thought about how that list had changed over the years. You make a change, live with it, and then move forward. It doesn't happen all at once.

Still, in the immortal words of Dorothy Parker, "I've never lived in Kiddletown, but I know I'd be just darling at it."

How not to be a robot

Pour-over coffee makes me laugh. The first time I saw someone in a cafe making pour-over coffee I thought maybe the power had gone out. This, after all, is how I made coffee when I was in college and could not afford a coffee maker. It's how you make coffee when you travel, or camp. It's that plastic or ceramic cone you take on vacation when the coffee machine where you're going might be skeevy. I'd say it's making a comeback, but in order to do that it has to have already been somewhere. I'm not even sure we had a word for it. Coffee cone? When I tried to look it up, I discovered it's been completely appropriated and is now a Pour Over Single Cup Brewing Cone.

Does it make a better cup of coffee? I can't honestly tell. It does take more time, which is perhaps how it earned its artisanal street cred. From where I sit, the thing that makes it better is that the person making it needs to pay attention to you for a little longer than usual. I like this trend.

Hopefully hot water bottles will follow suit. The last time I went looking for something like a hot water bottle, everything was fancy and pretty much useless. When I need the comfort of a hot water bottle, the microwave is already busy with my mac and cheese. Keep your lavender buckwheat and give me back my weird rubber smell – which is a lot better than when you accidentally set fire to your buckwheat wrap in the microwave.

Hot water bottles have all the hallmarks of the next big thing. They are super simple, sustainable, cheap, and relatively unheard of in current society. When I looked up how long they've been around (1903 if you're curious), I ran into questions about what a hot water bottle is for. They are for heating up your bed on a cold night, relaxing tense muscles, and relieving cramps. If you shuffle into the kitchen to fill your hot water bottle and shuffle away with it clutched to your abdomen, everyone in a five mile radius will leave you alone. And, like a pour over coffee cone, you can use a hot water bottle when the power goes out.

I can see carpooling being a thing again, too. When I was growing up my dad had a carpool. Not only did they share rides, but my sister tells me they pooled their resources and bought a second hand car together so their wives had use of the family cars. These men commuted together for decades, eventually all going to each others kids' weddings.

When my dad's office was moved across the country several of the families ended up in the same little mountain town and continued to carpool. They'd meet at the library, which shared a parking lot with the DMV and the open high school. The open high school was an alternative school for kids who weren't fitting into the public high school culture – mostly stoners, metal heads and poets. It's also where I had orchestra rehearsal in middle school. There were not a lot of kids who played violin at my school, so I was pretty self-conscious about carrying it around. I'd sneak into rehearsal past high schoolers lounging on bean bag chairs, hoping they were all gone when it was time to go. I remember hiding in the shrubbery in front of the school after several rehearsals waiting for my dad to pick me up on his way home, and then watching as he drove by. I knew I had about 20 minutes for him to get home, realize something was missing, and come back for me. I think about how crazy I was about my dad whenever Chris forgets to pick up the kids.

If you drive into Boston at commuting time, you'll notice that nearly everyone is driving alone. Even in the HOV lane few cars have more than two people in them. I know a lot of people are looking at jobs based on how easy it is to commute by bike or public transportation, but maybe the people who live farther out can make carpooling a thing again. It's like a book club, but with less wine.

I am not the most sociable person and love the convenience and don't-talk-to-me features of things like scanning my own groceries. We don't have to go to movies anymore because we can watch them at home. The grocery store delivers our food and anything else we need ships free with Amazon Prime. If you think about how much interaction we have lost, it's no wonder we want to linger a bit. Say what you will about Millennials, but around here the businesses they're creating are not only filling a niche, they're reintroducing us to human contact. As we lose more and more jobs to actual robots, human interaction will be the next big thing. And that human is pouring over my coffee.

How not to provide a bio and headshot

One year my sister decided that since I like to write and she doesn't, I should be her ghost writer. As a start, I was given the opportunity to write her bio for an upcoming high school reunion. I put it off until the very last possible moment, at which point she was essentially lying at my feet begging me to write the infernal thing. I emailed what I had, and then we IM'd out the details.

Her: Does there have to be so much about my goldfish?

Me: It's not a fish, it's a literary device. It moves the plot along.

Her: But an entire paragraph?

Me: *I loved that fish. The fish stays.*

Every so often I'm asked to submit a bio of my own. They are generally due the instant they are requested, which implies that most people getting these calls already have such things put together and ready to email. Or else they make a phone call and someone else emails them.

I have neither a bio nor a personal assistant. Every once in a while when I go shopping in uber-snobby places I like to say "I'll send my girl by later" and leave my parcels. I then call half a dozen friends to find someone to go get my stuff. Usually it's something like a new nail file because, hello? who do you think I am shopping in these places?

But I can't call and get a friend to email a bio when I don't have one, so I cobble something together. These bios run along the lines of "Susan is the trophy wife of record mogul Chris Blood. They live in the palatial Trout Towers, where musicians come and go, artists congregate and tea is served promptly." There will be no mention of chickens, bathroom fixtures in driveways or the seven vehicles routinely parked in the environs. And it will not specify exactly what we mean by "promptly." Or "mogul." Or even "trophy" for that matter. Perhaps I mean it in the bowling trophy sense. Who'd know?

In lieu of a bio, my editor at The Magazine of Yoga sent me an email one morning asking if there were a few salient points I'd like to include on the author page. I wrote:

"I'm really good at figuring out which container the leftover chili will fit in. I live in a recording studio. I write Trout Towers and a blog about opera. I really really want to play the opening chords of 'Back in Black' on electric guitar. I have never played electric guitar. Up until quite recently I had five chickens in my living room. I like lemon curd, have a knack for finding four leaf clovers and prefer to be called 'the iconic Susan Blood.'"

That entire piece of prose became my bio. Aside from the glaring omission of a reference to Sparky the goldfish, I think it still works.

How not to find a job

A few years ago a writer friend asked me what my plans were for my career. I didn't have an answer because I haven't planned for my career since I was in middle school, deciding I wanted to train wild animals. After that I wanted to be a photographer because apparently all girls at some point a) want a horse and b) want to be photographers. Given my experience with horses, I skipped straight to photography. I had exactly one exhibit of my photography, which was so awful it still makes me wince.

It's safe to say that I haven't planned my career so much as my career planned me. After college I took a job as a photographer at a ski resort because if you answer an ad in a ski town and arrive at twilight as all the twinkly lights are coming on and the mountains start to turn purpley blue, you will say yes to working for $6/hour and decide you have always wanted to live on Malt-O-Meal.

Likewise my move to the beach: Move first, juggle livelihood later. When I first moved to the east coast I answered an ad for art sales, since I had been managing an art gallery in Colorado. The interview went like this:

"Are you money-motivated?"

"I don't even know what that..."

"Be here at 8:00 a.m."

I went at 8:00 a.m. because what the heck and got in a car with a guy named Steve who drove me to Providence. This was before cell phones, so he quite easily could have left me there like a relocated mouse, but instead he handed me a stack of framed art prints – Degas' dancers, Monet's waterlilies, Renoir's Dance at Bougival – and told me to follow him. He led me in the direction of a huge office building, but missed the front door.

"I think the entrance is right over..."

"We're not using the entrance," he said. "We're gonna back door boogie."

We snuck in the back door, past security like a freaking scene from Mission Impossible and went from office to office, telling people we had overstock art from a building remodel next door and our boss told us to get rid of them.

He told me to let him do the talking. He must have instinctively known that my spiel would instantly devolve into "we picked these up in a warehouse this morning and I'm supposed to tell you that they came from a dentist office or something, which they didn't, but could you please buy them anyway so I can hurry home and cry in my tea?"

He had an answer for everything. No renovation next door? It was the building next to next door. Huge "no soliciting" sign? But we were sent here specifically at someone's request. Who was that someone? Can't remember, but you're welcome to call the office to get the details. Eventually, security was called. Something must have gone off in Steve's in-ear monitor because suddenly he's pushing prints into my arms and shoving me toward the stairwell.

"Oops! We left the box of Norman Rockwells next to the water cooler," I tell him, and turn to retrieve our stock. He blocks my way.

"Go, go, go, go, GO!" he hisses, taking five stairs at a time. We stopped on the third floor and loitered in a broom closet until the coast was clear.

Eventually he realized that having Pollyanna as a sidekick was slowing him down and he offloaded me in a park with a turkey sandwich. On the way back he said, "maybe you'd do best in the office. I think we need someone to run the office." I agreed.

I never called them. They – astonishingly – did not call me.

If you've ever sat on the floor in front of a case of Encyclopedia Brittanica unable to stop looking things up, you understand that this also happens when you start looking up words in dictionaries. And so I bring you

Career:

1a. A chosen pursuit; a profession or occupation.

1b. The general course or progression of one's working life or one's professional achievements: an officer with a distinguished career; a teacher in the midst of a long career.

2. A path or course, as of the sun through the heavens. (www.thefreedictionary.com)

Guidance never mentioned a path through the heavens, but that's what I think it should feel like. So I let my career search guide me across the country, and back. When I returned to Colorado I landed in Denver and registered with an employment agency, where I submitted a resumé and awaited a cornucopia of available job choices. By this time I had been a manager of two art galleries, spoke three languages, and knew how to spell. I am incredibly hireable, with excellent references. Anyone in their right mind would want to work with me.

"There are no jobs that fit your skills," my employment agent said.

"You mean there are none available?" I clarified.

"No."

It seems I had reached a point in life where I had no useful skills and my liberal arts degree was not helping. So I did what I do best: I went through the paper, circled everything that didn't physically make me want to vomit, and applied for jobs.

I found a bunch of little jobs, but nothing that screamed "write home and tell mom about this," so I called the place I most wanted to work and asked if they needed a volunteer. They didn't, but the woman I spoke to asked for my number and within the hour an organization she contacted called to ask if I'd come help them.

Volunteering is great because it keeps you in the field you love, no matter what you're doing to pay the rent. At the end of the day, it's what you contribute that's important. It's that simple. Are you contributing? Are you happy doing it? When we choose our career paths, we're choosing what we're good at - except that's not something many of us choose. It's something we discover. The problem is that "career" is a noun, but it works best as a verb. Unless you do something about it, a career is either wishful thinking or a careening series of paychecks. To figure out what it is you're supposed to be doing, listen to people who tell you when you're on the right track. Listen to the message until you know it's true, and then start practicing whatever it is.

Just as I realized I had worked in the arts for 10 years, with a progression of jobs that looked almost intentional, a colleague suggested we throw it all to the wind and move to Cape Cod.

"Absolutely not," I said.

A month later my adorable apartment building was sold and we all had a month to move out. Faced with the need to find a new apartment down the street, I packed it up, threw it all to the wind, and moved to Cape Cod.

In other parts of the country, if you have more than one job you aren't making it. On Cape Cod if you only have one job people assume you're lazy or there is something wrong with you. This is great because sometimes the thing you most want to do doesn't pay all your bills yet. Over time, the work you're aiming for starts to take hold, and you can peel off the extras. It's like shedding floatation devices when you're learning to swim. Do whatever you need to do to make it possible to fulfill your job on this planet.

I don't remember what we were doing when my friend asked if I had heard about "be, do, have" because as soon as she started explaining it I forgot everything else. I also hit myself really hard in the head because it is so very, very obvious I really should have thought it up all by myself. In retrospect, I recommend the idea-stealing more than the head-hitting.

"Be, do, have" is a process that many of us approach in the wrong order. If you aspire to be something or do something specific with your life, you follow this process which is a mobius strip of action. There is not a point at which you are done. You start with being. You may be a writer or a ballerina or a toymaker elf dentist, but whatever you are, you must be it. You know it in your core. It is who you are.

Next, you do. If you are a writer, you write. If you are a ballerina, you take ballet lessons. If you are a toymaker elf dentist, you practice dentistry. You don't let anyone bully you into being what you are not. Nor do you let yourself bully you into being less than what you are. This is your practice. In the case of the elf dentist, you fix all the teeth of all the toys and then you go out into the world and continue your practice. You may find yourself (spoiler alert) called upon to do some Very Big Things with Very Big Teeth. This will not phase you, because remember? You're a dentist.

After being and doing comes having. You have a career. You have awards. You have a necklace of Abominable Snow Monster Teeth which gives you lower back pain when you wear it but, damn it's cool. At some point in the having process, you may forget who you are and need to go back to being – which never actually stopped. You also need to keep practicing because laurels are uncomfortable when you sit on them.

The Holy Grail of work is to do all this from home. Working from home is proof that you know what you're doing and don't need supervision. You excel at time management. Your track record of being reliable, efficient and on time allows you to set your own hours. For me, working from home is the perfect scenario and its own little slice of hell.

Everything you read about how to manage a writing practice says to get into a routine. To write at a certain time each day, without fail. Most claim to do it in the morning when they're fresh, before the demands of the day eat up all the other hours. The idea is that you get into a groove. You have a series of things you do: Get up, make coffee, write. Once you are in the groove, you find yourself inexplicably settling into work with your hot cup of coffee because it's what you *do*. This works for a lot of people.

It does not work for me. I have an anti-addictive personality. I try to be a methodical creature of habit, but it just doesn't take. That TV show I'm addicted to? I forget and watch it a month late. There is no groove carved deep enough to keep me from wandering out of it.

Even if I set a time to work and get myself to sit down at my computer, I still can't seem to focus on the task at hand. The most mundane job has me running to Facebook in a panic. If I close Facebook I end up scrolling through images on Google to see which era of Billy Corgan's hair my son is reminding me of at the moment. I limp along this way until I notice that my laptop is at 23%, at which point I realize I have frittered away 77% of my battery life on goat videos and am now earning $4.50 an hour. This is when I take my laptop and move away from my power cable. I may not be a creature of habit, but I am absolutely a creature of comfort and once I am

Thank you.

I am so grateful for everyone who appears in this book except possibly the mice. Endless thanks to Rob Conery, without whose faith and daring this never would have happened. Thank you to Michael and Suz Karchmer for taking 500 photographs of my feet, and to Kristen vonHentschel for making them into the cover. Thank you to Marilee McKelvey and Robert Junker for catching my split infinitives and farther/furthers, and to Susan and Margo Maier-Moul for letting me write for The Magazine of Yoga while not making me do actual yoga. Love to Jud, Joyce and Jennifer, always.